CLOSED-END FUND PRICING

Theories and Evidence

Innovations in Financial Markets and Institutions

Editor:

Mark Flannery
University of Florida

Other books in the series:

Hoshi, Takeo and Patrick, Hugh:
Crisis and Change in the Japanese Financial System
Cummins, J. David and Santomero, Anthony M.:
Changes in the Life Insurance Industry: Efficiency, Technology and Risk Management
Barron, J.M., and Staten, M.E.:
Credit Life Insurance: A Re-Examination of Policy and Practice
Cottrell, A.F., Lawlor, M.S., Wood, J.H.:
The Causes and Costs of Depository Institution Failures
Anderson, S., Beard, T.R., Born, J.:
Initial Public Offerings: Findings and Theories
Anderson, S., and Born, J.:
Closed-End Investment Companies
Kaufman, G.:
Banking Structures in Major Countries
England, C.:
Governing Banking's Future
Hancock, D.:
A Theory of Production for the Financial Firm
Gup, B.:
Bank Mergers: Current Issues and Perspectives

CLOSED-END FUND PRICING

Theories and Evidence

Seth C. Anderson
Department of Accounting and Finance
University of North Florida

Jeffery A. Born
College of Business Administration
Northeastern University

KLUWER ACADEMIC PUBLISHERS
Boston / Dordrecht / London

Distributors for North, Central and South America:
Kluwer Academic Publishers
101 Philip Drive
Assinippi Park
Norwell, Massachusetts 02061 USA
Telephone (781) 871-6600
Fax (781) 681-9045
E-Mail <kluwer@wkap.com>

Distributors for all other countries:
Kluwer Academic Publishers Group
Distribution Centre
Post Office Box 322
3300 AH Dordrecht, THE NETHERLANDS
Telephone 31 78 6392 392
Fax 31 78 6546 474
E-Mail <services@wkap.nl>

Electronic Services <http://www.wkap.nl>
ISBN 978-1-4419-4940-0

Library of Congress Cataloging-in-Publication Data

A C.I.P. Catalogue record for this book is available
from the Library of Congress.

Printed on acid-free paper.

Printed in the United States of America

Dedication

This book is dedicated to our children:
Lela, Frank, and Richard Anderson of Ponte Vedra Beach, Florida;
Sarah, Jeffery, and Megan Born of Hingham, Massachusetts.

Contents

Acknowledgements

We wish to express appreciation to Professor Mark Flannery of the University of Florida, who supported our proposal to update our previous work in this area. We also thank David Cella, Judith Pforr, and Denise Gibson at Kluwer for their assistance and patience. The completion of the book was greatly facilitated by the editorial work of Linda Anderson and the word processing of Emilie Espanet and Vincent Shea. We are most thankful to our patient families.

Preface

Closed-End Investment Companies (CEICs) were the first investor-owned organizations that pooled and invested funds primarily, if not exclusively, in financial assets. First developed on the Continent in the early 19th century, this type of organization later flourished in Victorian England and Scotland, where investment trusts are still popular today. That early popularity spread, as the first U.S. closed-end funds were formed in the late 19th century and peaked in popularity during the late 1920s.

In contrast, the first open-end fund, Massachusetts Investors Trust, was formed in 1924. It was another twenty years before the net value of assets under management at open-end funds exceeded those under management at closed-end funds. Thereafter, open-end funds grew rapidly while CEICs stagnated.

After decades of indifference and obscurity new life was breathed into the industry starting about 1985. Both the number of new funds created and capital raised by these funds reached a record peak in 1993. The resurgence of closed-end funds was, in part, responsible for our desire to write the first book: *Closed-End Investment Companies: Issues and Answers.*

Closed-end funds differ from open-end funds in two important aspects, which are discussed in greater detail in a later chapter. First, the funds do not stand willing to repurchase their outstanding shares from their owners, as do open-end funds. Second, the funds do not continuously engage in a primary offering of their shares. They tend to issue shares only once, and changes in ownership are achieved in the secondary market, like the vast majority of other securities transactions. Interestingly, CEIC share prices do not necessarily equal their net asset value (NAV) per share. This apparent "anomaly" has been the focus of an extensive amount of academic research over the past fifty years.

In ***CLOSED-END FUND PRICING: Theories and Evidence***, we attempt to summarize the academic articles that have come to print since the publication of our first work in 1992. We also include some older pieces that we missed in our prior work. We review only academic articles in print, as the location of dissertations and working papers would be very difficult. This second book covers 61 works, nearly twice the number of articles that we reviewed previously. Because of the increase in articles, we are unable to reproduce numerical findings with the same detail that we did in the first book. We apologize in advance for any oversight of works.

Chapter 1

AN INTRODUCTION TO INVESTMENT COMPANIES

As with our first volume, we believe that it is appropriate to begin this volume with an overview of the Investment Company Act of 1940 and the 1950 amendments to that act. This legislation controls the activity of closed-end and open-end investment companies. Those readers who are familiar with these acts may wish to go directly to Chapter 2. Investment companies are the dominant vehicles for channeling the savings of U.S. investors into financial assets, here and abroad. As of January 2000, the amount of assets under management by these organizations was estimated to be $12 trillion, or about $50,000 for every man, woman, and child in the United States.

1. MANAGEMENT GUIDELINES

Corporate Entity. The Act of 1940 requires an investment company to be a domestic corporation or a domestic entity taxed as a corporation. This provision rules out personal holding companies attempting to qualify for the favourable tax treatment of income under the act. The company must be registered as a management company or a unit investment trust, as defined by the act, at all times during the year when the favourable tax treatment is claimed.

Management Contracts. The investment management franchise cannot be sold to another entity once the company has been chartered. Removal of the investment management contract from the sponsor is possible, provided the motion receives a favourable vote from the shareholders. The investment managers are strictly prohibited from any self-dealing with the firm. In essence, these provisions commit management to a long-term fiduciary obligation to the stockholders, as well as reduce the probability of fraud.

Board of Directors. At least 40% of the Board of Directors must be non-officers or advisors to the fund. Investment brokers or the company's regular brokers may not constitute a majority of the Board. These provisions ensure that a majority of the Board's members are financially independent of the fund.

2. INVESTMENT POLICY GUIDELINES

Income Sources. At least 90% of an investment company's gross income must be passive income (i.e., dividends, interest, and/or gains from the sale of securities). This provision ensures that the non-investment activities of the fund do not contribute to its revenues. For any taxable year, a maximum of 30% of the fund's profits can be derived from the sale of securities held for less than three months (before deducting short-term trading losses, but including all short- and long-term gains from the short-sale of securities). This latter provision discourages investment companies from speculating on short-term fluctuations in security prices.

Portfolio Composition. The Act of 1940 requires that at the end of each quarter during the taxable year, the fund must: (a) have at least 50% of its assets in cash, cash items (including receivables), government securities, securities of other regulated investment companies, or other financial assets; (b) limit its investment in any single security to 5% or less of its total assets; (c) not have an investment in any single company that represents more than 10% of the outstanding voting securities of the issuer; (d) limit its investment in the securities of any one issuer (except government securities or the securities of other regulated funds) to 25% or less of its total assets; and (e) limit its investment in the securities of two or more controlled (defined as 20% ownership of outstanding voting securities) companies in the same or similar line of business to 25% or less of the total assets of the fund. These restrictions are designed to keep funds from becoming vehicles for controlling other firms or real assets. The Real Estate Investment Trust (REIT) Act of 1960 provides guidelines for the creation of investment companies that wish to invest in real estate or real estate-based financial assets, paving the way for REITs.

Investment Policy Statement. Upon the initial organization of a fund, or the effective date of the Act of 1940 for funds in existence at that time, a statement of the investment policies and objectives must be provided. This statement addresses in general terms the kinds of financial assets in which the fund will invest, the kinds of risks that will be undertaken, the fund's planned use of leverage, etc. Once in place, an investment policy cannot be changed without a majority vote of the shareholders. The purpose of the policy statement is to help potential investors assess the risks they would face as shareholders of the fund, and to ensure that management does not suddenly change these risks.

3. CAPITAL STRUCTURE GUIDELINES

Minimum Equity Capital. If the firm desires to make a public offering of its common shares, it must have at least $100,000 of equity capital. A prospectus that discloses the information required by the Act of 1940 must accompany any public offering.

Senior Security Limitation. At least three times total assets must cover an investment company's funded debt. At least two times total assets must cover preferred stock issued by the fund. These provisions are designed to create a large margin of safety for the senior security holders of the fund, should it be forced into receivership or bankruptcy.

4. TAX POLICIES

If a variety of tests are met, the net profits of investment companies are themselves exempt from federal income taxation. Distribution of income from tax-exempt (taxable) sources is most likely tax-exempt (taxable) for the recipient. The provisions are designed to create an organization that is a "conduit" through which passive income can flow to its shareholders.

Dividend and Interest Income. To retain an investment company's tax-exempt status, a fund must distribute no less than 90% of its net income, exclusive of capital gains. Under the 1950 amendments, dividend and interest income from one fiscal year may be paid in the following fiscal year without jeopardizing the status of the fund. The tax status is maintained as long as the distributions are declared no later than the due date of the fund's tax return and are paid no later than the first regular dividend date following the declaration. Regardless of the source (dividends or interest), distributions are treated as dividend income by the stockholder. These provisions provide funds with an opportunity to delay the declaration and distribution of dividends about one quarter (or a little more if the normal distribution policy of the fund is semi-annual or annual, and the fund follows a calendar fiscal year and files taxes by April 15th).

Capital Gains. To retain an investment company's tax-exempt status, a fund must distribute 100% of net capital gains in a manner and form similar to the one described above. Sub-chapter M of the Act of 1940 permits a fund to retain recognized capital gains without losing its investment company status (and thus, its tax-exempt status on net dividend and interest income). However, electing to retain capital gains leads to a capital gain tax liability that is computed at the maximum possible rate. Although retention is rare, any tax paid by the company would be passed on to stockholders as a tax credit on a pro-rata basis. Clearly this provision is designed to encourage, but not require, funds to be a passive conduit for capital gains.

5. TYPES OF INVESTMENT COMPANIES

Open-End Funds. Common shares of an open-end investment company are purchased directly from the fund in a primary market transaction. Purchases may be made through a properly licensed broker, or may be made directly from the fund (e.g., through a dividend re-investment plan). Security regulations require that a prospectus be made available to potential investors prior to the sale. A prospectus is a highly stylized document that contains up-to-date information. The prospectus details the investment philosophy of the fund, assesses the risks of that philosophy, and discloses management fee schedules, dividend re-investment policies, share redemption policies, sales and/or redemption fees, the past performance of the fund, the minimum initial and subsequent investment (dollar) amounts, etc. It is the sale of new shares and redemption policies of open-end funds that distinguish them from closed-end funds.

Closed-End Funds. Licensed brokers generally offer the shares of a new closed-end fund to the public. Additional offerings of new shares by public closed-end funds are rare. Closed-end funds invest the initial offering's proceeds, less floatation costs, in accordance with the investment policy statement found in the prospectus. Closed-end funds do not continuously engage in a primary offering of common stock. Except for self-liquidating closed-end funds, which are quite rare, the organizations do not have a redemption policy. Changes in ownership of outstanding shares of closed-end funds are undertaken in secondary market transactions on the exchange (e.g., NYSE) on which the fund's shares are listed.

The price at which secondary market transactions for shares of closed-end funds take place has no necessary relation to the net asset value (NAV) per share of the fund. The NAV is defined as the market (or appraised value) of the fund's assets, less the fund's liabilities (and total par value of any preferred shares outstanding), divided by the number of common shares outstanding. While shares can sell above and below their NAV, the majority of funds' shares usually sell at a price below their respective NAV. The fact that closed-end fund share price and NAV differ frequently has made these organizations the focus of much attention in academic and investment communities for decades. This academic literature is the subject of our two monographs.

Chapter 2

A BRIEF OVERVIEW OF THE CLOSED-END FUND INDUSTRY

In our first volume we present an abbreviated history of the development of closed-end funds (CEICs), touching several of the pioneering organizations. Here, we provide a brief overview of the closed-end fund industry in the United States. We attempt this via a brief history and some statistics about CEICs currently existing. We caution that some information prior to 1950 is difficult to obtain. In addition, organizations that were once considered "funds" or "trusts" would no longer be considered as such under the Investment Company Act of 1940 or its 1950 amendments. We have made every effort to be accurate in the compilation of the following data.

1. BRIEF HISTORY

There is debate about the origins of the first closed-end investment company in the United States. Until the late 19th century, many trusts and corporations in the United States had limited lives or self-liquidation clauses that disbanded the entity and distributed its capital once its stated objectives were met. As a result, it is difficult to determine when or where the first chartered organization accepted, pooled, and invested contributors' funds for their benefit.

Depending upon how broadly one defines "pooling of resources" and contributors' "benefit," the formation of closed-end fund-like enterprises extends back to the earliest settlement of what was to become the United States. Both the Plymouth Colony charter (1621) and Massachusetts Bay Colony charter (1629) created organizations for the benefit of the Crown and the settlers. For example, within the Massachusetts Bay Colony, Hingham (1635) was organized as a "plantation" where ungranted/untitled lands were distributed to property holders in accordance with the number of "shares" homesteads owned. Early town records contain entries which describe debates over what properties constituted a full share and who really owned which properties.

Leaving these more distant examples behind, some argue that the Massachusetts Hospital Life Insurance Company (formed 1823) is the forerunner of closed-end funds, while others identify the New York Stock Trust (formed 1889), the Boston Personal Property Trust (formed 1893), or the Alexander Fund (formed 1907), as candidates. The Massachusetts Hospital Life Insurance Company was liquidated well before 1900. However, at least two funds existed at that time.

It is unclear how rapidly closed-end funds grew in the early 20th century, and it was 1928 when the NYSE allowed closed-end funds to be listed. While a number of firms chose to be listed, many did not. Reporting investment results to investors was infrequent, unregulated, and haphazard, at best. Ironically, as stock prices began to collapse in late 1929, a number of CEICs began reporting financial results -- possibly in an effort to "signal" their quality and/or in an effort to stem their rapidly declining share prices. Unfortunately, a large number of the funds made use of extensive leverage and were wiped out when the stock market collapsed.

Subsequent to the Investment Company Act of 1940, information about the risks, returns, and portfolios held by investment companies has increased and has been standardized. From the end of World War II until the mid-60s, few new closed-end funds were formed. However, in the years 1965-1999, at least 54 closed-end funds ceased operations -- either converting to an open-end format or by liquidating. While the number of CEICs ceasing operations is rather small, the number of funds created since the mid-60s is much larger.

2. RECENT FUND STATISTICS

To complete an overview of closed-end funds, Table 2.1 presents 13 non-overlapping fund groups based on fund objective. Many funds invest primarily in equities, ranging from small cap equities to preferred securities. Others are bond-oriented, investing in debt securities ranging in quality from treasuries to junk status.

Prior to 1985 only a few funds targeted other country markets. Table 2.1 reveals that currently there are approximately 170 different funds that target non-U.S. markets, some investing in securities of a single country while others invest globally. The so-called world income funds are an interesting development. These bond funds often try to take advantage of "segmented" capital markets, investing in portfolios of bonds that appear to have yields well in excess of what is implied by their risk characteristics.

Table2.1 **Closed-End Funds by Category with Average Premium as of 2/16/01**

Category	Number	Average Premium
General Equity Funds	25	- 2.33%
Specialized Equity Funds	20	- 9.15%
Income and Preferred Stock Funds	12	- 3.25%
Convertible Securities Funds	9	- 3.98%
World Equity Funds	70	-16.86%
Total Equity Funds	*136*	*-10.87%*
U.S. Government Funds	6	- 6.45%
U.S. Mortgage Bond Funds	20	- 4.45%
Investment Grade Bond Funds	14	- 3.67%
Loan Participation Funds	40	+ 1.86%
High Yield Bond Funds	33	+11.27%
Other Domestic Taxable Bond Funds	29	- 2.40%
World Income/ National Municipal Bond Funds	100	- 5.49%
Single State Bond Funds	115	- 4.00%
Total Bond Funds	*357*	*- 2.60%*
Total Closed-End Funds	***493***	***- 5.21%***

[illegible] 1995 [illegible]

Table [illegible] Average [illegible]

Category	[illegible]	[illegible]
[illegible]	[illegible]	[illegible]
[illegible]	[illegible]	[illegible]
[illegible]	[illegible]	[illegible]
[illegible]	[illegible]	[illegible]
[illegible]	[illegible]	[illegible]
[illegible]	[illegible]	[illegible]
[illegible]	[illegible]	[illegible]
U.S. Government [illegible]	[illegible]	[illegible]
U.S. [illegible]	[illegible]	[illegible]
[illegible]	[illegible]	[illegible]
[illegible]	[illegible]	[illegible]
High [illegible]	[illegible]	[illegible]
Other [illegible] Bond [illegible]	[illegible]	[illegible]
World [illegible]		
[illegible]	[illegible]	[illegible]
[illegible]	[illegible]	[illegible]
Total [illegible]	[illegible]	[illegible]
Total [illegible]	[illegible]	[illegible]

Chapter 3

CONTENT SUMMARIES OF VOLUMES ONE AND TWO

1. RESEARCH EVOLUTION

The growth of an academic literature in a topic area does not proceed like a flow of lava or like the waves that emanate when a stone is tossed into a smooth body of water. The progression is more like the evolving of a species or the growth of a family tree. Modern life sciences document numerous jumps in evolution, and anyone seeing a family tree knows that some branches are bare sticks, whereas others develop into diverse bodies. In short, the growth of an academic literature is bumpy, uneven, and erratic.

In the ten years since our original publication, closed-end fund articles have addressed new areas and revisited old ones. This literature appears in both established and newer academic journals. Obviously, the recent growth of electronic databases provides researchers with the ability to engage in relatively low-cost searches, thereby facilitating new research. This is manifest in the approximate 65 articles from the recent decade reviewed in our current work, compared to the 35 articles of which we are aware that appeared prior to 1991.

2. TOPICS COVERED IN VOLUME ONE

In our first volume we review all of the closed-end fund academic literature in print up to the date of its publication in 1992. The review follows two short chapters that provide an overview of the legislation regulating the activities of investment companies and a brief history of closed-end investment companies (CEICs). The primary findings are briefly summarized in the following paragraphs.

Most closed-end funds' shares exhibit prices lower than their calculated net asset value (NAV). These so-called "discounts" can be substantial, long-lasting, and variable, and are, perhaps, the most interesting aspect of closed-end investment companies. Much of the academic literature prior to 1990 is devoted to explaining the magnitude and persistence in CEIC discounts. The below hypothesized factors are discussed in detail in our first volume.

Unrealized capital appreciation in the portfolio of a closed-end fund raises the possibility that it will be recognized, the gain distributed (in order to maintain the tax-exempt status of the fund), and the stockholder will pay taxes on these gains. However, the distribution of gains should reduce the price and NAV of the fund, dollar for dollar, whereas the investor will retain only (1 - T)% of the distributed gain, where T is the marginal tax rate expressed as a decimal. Malkiel (1977) argues that investors will discount the price of the closed-end fund shares to compensate for their tax liability on the gain.

In addition to the unrecognized capital appreciation issue, it is often argued that the frequency at which gains are realized and distributed impacts discounts. Some contend that a frequent recognition and distribution policy should minimize the amount of unrecognized gains and thus, the fund's discount. Pre-Miller and Modigliani (1961), some argue that low-tax/high-tax investors prefer a frequent/infrequent distribution of gains, respectively. Depending upon the fund's shareholder mix, a discount/premium could develop based on the net dissatisfaction/satisfaction with the fund's distribution policy.

However, in a perfect capital market with no transactions costs, funds would act as a transparent conduit through which dividends and interest received would be passed along to shareholders. In our world, with its attendant transactions costs, most funds employ a quarterly payout policy. Some authors argue that infrequent/frequent distributions will increase/decrease discounts because firms do not directly pass along the short-term returns on the income between quarterly payments. While technically accurate, only under the most extreme portfolio assumptions could this factor explain the level of discounts frequently observed for CEICs. While the two above factors do not appear to have much, if any, ability to explain the pattern of observed discounts, these suppositions provide an underpinning of the "tax-timing" extensions that are covered in this volume.

In a different vein, a number of authors contend that transactions costs impact fund discounts. Some argue that small investors can save on commissions by purchasing shares of a closed-end fund compared to the costs incurred in replicating the fund's portfolio. This should lead to a premium for funds. Conversely, they argue that management fees reduce the cash flows to the shareholders of closed-end funds, which should produce a discount. Finally, some authors argue that funds sell at discounts when their managers engage in excessive portfolio turnover. In summary, these transactions cost-like arguments usually translate into a predicted discount for the fund, but their magnitude can rarely justify the discounts generally observed.

Additionally, other factors related to a fund's portfolio are often argued to impact discounts. The holding of large blocks, restricted shares, or an undiversified portfolio is held by some to increase fund discounts. Alternately, the relation between foreign asset holdings and discounts is uncertain: the added risks of foreign securities is argued to have negative influence, while the diversification benefits of foreign assets is thought to have a positive influence. Although the influence of these factors on discounts is generally upheld by empirical analysis, the relative size of the impact is frequently inconsistent with an economic interpretation of the data.

Yet, others offer a number of factors that do not rely on a rational model of value to explain the discounts on closed-end funds. These "irrational" factors include: market inefficiency, investor sentiment, level of the market, past performance, illiquid trading, no sales effort as compared to open-end funds, and/or the listing market (NYSE, ASE, or NASDAQ). Although there is some evidence that the lack of sales efforts might influence discounts, this does not explain the magnitude of discounts usually observed. Also, there is not enough variability in efforts/commission rates to explain the volatility of discounts. In the prior volume, we find no evidence to conclude that discounts forecast the future performance of the fund or that they are a result of past performance. However, new research in this arena may temper these findings.

After reviewing 36 articles in the first volume, we conclude that the research yields a number of rational factors that partially explain closed-end fund discounts. While no single factor appears to explain the existence of and variability of closed-end fund discounts, we find no reason to abandon rational-based models for those that invoke irrationality.

In a different vein, the earlier literature also reveals evidence of serial correlation in short-term changes in fund prices and that discounts have mean-reverting characteristics. These two aspects of CEIC behavior contribute to the profitability of trading rules constructed on discounts. Additionally, evidence is presented that closed-end funds' IPOs are not underpriced (i.e., first day returns are much lower than for other types of stock offerings), and that funds perform poorly following the IPO. Subsequent research continues to support these earlier findings.

3. TOPICS COVERED IN VOLUME TWO

Here we review the academic literature that has been published since our first volume. Also, we are aware of certain articles that were overlooked in our first volume, and we review them here, even though they were written before 1990. Some of the articles focus on a single topic; while others address multiple topics. We have assigned each article to one of four chapters for review. The four chapters are: (1) Discounts as an Index of Sentiment, (2) Closed-End Country Funds and International Diversification, (3) Other Efforts to Explain Closed-End Fund Discounts, and (4) Idiosyncratic Closed-End Funds Studies.

3.1 Discounts as an Index of Sentiment

In the early 1990s, there appeared a series of articles by a group of authors who argue that discounts on closed-end funds (CEICs) represent an index of investor sentiment. Building on the work of De Long, Shleifer, Summers and Waldman (1990), these papers posit that capital market participants can be placed into one of two categories: (A) those who are informed, rational, economic agents, and (B) those who are small, under-informed, and who suffer from periods of irrationality (i.e., "noise traders").

It is held that when institutional constraints cause trading in a security or market sector to be dominated by noise traders, price volatility rises and the informational efficiency of prices declines. Deviations from an efficient equilibrium can be pronounced and prolonged if the normal forces of arbitrage are absent or discouraged because of the irrational price swings allegedly produced by noise traders.

However, there appears to be limited institutional ownership of shares in closed-end funds because this would result in clients' paying a managerial fee for both the institution and the CEIC. In addition, few closed-end funds are taken over or converted to open-end fund status. Some conclude from this evidence that noise traders must dominate the trading in closed-end funds.

Some argue that the discounts on closed-end funds are the "price" that must be paid (by sellers of shares at less than their NAV) in order to induce investors to take on the systematic risk posed by the irrational noise traders. These authors hold that the average discount on CEICs provides a measure of the sentiment/mood of noise traders. Further, these authors provide some evidence that changes in the level of closed-end fund discounts are related to the returns earned on other investment vehicles that are thought to be attractive to noise traders.

3.2 Closed-End Country Funds and International Diversification

In the late 1980s and early 1990s, a wave of new closed-end fund offerings hit the U.S. capital markets. These funds came to market in response to growing investor interest in foreign investments. The bulk of the new funds were single country funds, which invest in the financial assets of firms traded in a single country (e.g. the Mexico Fund). Today, most countries in the world with financial markets have at least one closed-end country fund investing primarily in its markets. Another group of country funds limits their investments to a geographic region (e.g., Pacific Rim Fund). Yet, others invest in industries in a geographic region (e.g., Latin America Telecommunications Fund), while others invest anywhere (e.g., Global Fund).

Modern portfolio theory holds that the desirability of a financial asset is related to its expected return and the impact it has on the variability of a well-diversified portfolio held by a rational investor. A number of studies demonstrate the lack of correlation in returns earned by foreign financial assets and those earned by U.S. financial assets. As a result, efficient portfolio frontiers estimated with foreign and U.S. financial assets usually offer higher returns at each level of risk (dominate) than do frontiers estimated with only U.S. financial assets.

A number of issues regarding country funds and international diversification have been examined. One issue is the ability of closed-end funds to deliver the diversification benefits offered by direct investments in the underlying foreign securities. In addition, some studies address the performance of closed-end fund investments and how this relates to exchange rate risk, the quality of investment management, the variability of closed-end fund discounts, and the performance of the underlying foreign market.

Many studies demonstrate the benefit to U.S. investors of direct foreign portfolio diversification. Others demonstrate that closed-end funds are imperfect vehicles for delivering diversification benefits. There is little agreement on why foreign portfolio investment benefits and closed-end country fund investment benefits differ. However, some studies report evidence of U.S. markets influencing the returns to country fund shareholders. This influence may lessen the potential reduction in variability of returns if country funds, rather than direct foreign investments, are added to a portfolio of U.S. financial assets.

3.3 Other Efforts to Explain Closed-End Fund Discounts

A number of pieces in the past decade re-examine the ability of one or more "rational" factors to explain cross-sectional deviations in closed-end fund discounts. The more recent studies seek to improve previous definitions, measures, and proxies for theoretical constructs related to CEICs' discounts. The large increase in the number of CEICs presents a rich database for re-examining prior hypotheses.

Four factors receive considerable attention in the recent closed-end fund literature: (1) expenses, (2) tax-timing options, (3) management performance, and (4) management ownership. All make contributions to the literature, but none fully explains discounts. However, among others, one intriguing finding is the strength of the cross-sectional relation between discounts and future portfolio performance of the fund.

3.4 Idiosyncratic Closed-End Fund Studies

In addition to the three groups of new studies listed above, there are a number of closed-end funds studies that defy classification into a common group. Many of the works contained in this fourth section represent single themes and may spawn the growth of a body of work in subsequent years. Hopefully, our review of these pieces can help facilitate research in these areas.

Chapter 4

CLOSED-END FUND DISCOUNTS AS AN INVESTOR SENTIMENT INDEX

1. INTRODUCTION

Possibly the earliest discussion of investor sentiment, albeit unnamed, occurred during the run-up in U.S. stocks in the spring and summer of 1929 when closed-end funds mostly sold at substantial premiums to their net asset value (see De Long and Shliefer (1991)). These early writers were involved in brokerage or portfolio management, and they were warning investors that paying premiums of 100% or more was to pay twice or more the market value for the fund's assets. The writers were puzzled by the demand for closed-end funds and were quick to point out the superior performance that fund managers would have to achieve in order to justify the lofty premiums.

More recently, Charles M.C. Lee, Andrei Shleifer, and Richard Thaler (1991) published a pair of articles laying the framework for the hypothesis that the discounts on closed-end funds serve as an index of investor sentiment. The first article is in the *Journal of Economic Perspectives,* and the second, more formal, treatment is in the *Journal of Finance*. Two papers by J. Bradford De Long and Andrei Schleifer that are more historical in perspective follow Lee, et al. (1990). These four works constitute the primary underpinnings for the investor sentiment hypothesis.

The authors individually address and subsequently dismiss a host of "rationally-based" factors that are frequently offered to explain closed-end fund discounts. They contend that the only factor consistent with the levels of and behavior of closed-end fund discounts over time, and the pattern of closed-end fund IPOs, is investor sentiment. They argue that discounts are not a function of some causal factor, but that discounts are a measure of investor sentiment.

While not sufficient to produce discounts, the existence of small "noise traders" as hypothesized by this group of papers appears to be a necessary condition. The authors contend that the irrational behavior of these investors could be ignored (diversified away) if their influence were limited to a single class of assets or a small segment of the market. However, they present evidence that changes in the level of closed-end fund discounts are related to the returns on "small" stocks, and argue that the risk is systematic. If the risk is systematic, there must be compensation for those who bear it. Thus, they argue that the discounts from net asset value on closed-end funds are the compensation for this risk.

Shortly following this group of papers, several other studies take exception to the investor sentiment hypothesis. These articles find only marginal explanatory power of 4%-7% for the notion that noise traders provide an explanation for closed-end fund discounts. The debate between these two schools of thought is intense and continues currently. It is this process of testing and retesting hypotheses that drives the advancement of science.

Lee, Charles M.C., Adrei Shleifer, and Richard H. Thaler.
"Anomalies: Closed-End Mutual Funds." *Journal of Economic Perspectives* 4.4 (Fall 1990): 153-164.

This is the first of a series of articles to appear in this journal which addresses apparent violations of the efficient market hypothesis. The authors first discuss the variability of and persistence of discounts on closed-end funds. They review a variety of "rational" explanations for these deviations between the share price and net asset value of closed-end funds. They also consider the explanations that have been offered for the behavior of closed-end fund share prices soon after their initial public offering.

After moving through the normal set of "standard excuses" that are frequently offered to explain the apparent violation of the law of one price: agency costs, restricted stock ownership, and unrecognized capital gains, the authors conclude that these theories are ineffective or incomplete. They note that opening up closed-end funds causes discounts to virtually vanish overnight. The authors also argue that prior theories are unable to explain waves in IPOs of this type of security. They conclude with the argument that the behavior of noise traders in response to changes in their sentiment/outlook may provide an explanation for the level and variability of closed-end fund discounts and for the cyclical pattern of closed-end fund IPOs. The paper anticipates empirical findings that are reported subsequently.

Lee, Charles M. C., Andrei Shleifer, and Richard H. Thaler.
"Investor Sentiment and the Closed-End Fund Puzzle."
Journal of Finance 66.1 (March 1991): 75-109.

Here, the authors argue that changes in the level of discounts on seasoned funds and cycles in offerings of new closed-end funds can be explained by fluctuations in the level of investor sentiment. They critically analyze and reject three popular theories for explaining closed-end fund discounts: agency costs (e.g., excessive management fees), unrealized capital gains, and illiquid assets in the fund's portfolio. The authors contend that the level of these frictions is not sufficient to explain the large discounts that are frequently observed on seasoned funds, and, moreover, these frictions are too stable to explain the wide fluctuations that are observed in discounts at the fund level.

They offer the notion of noise trader sentiment as an explanation for the level of and variability of closed-end fund discounts. It is argued that noise traders make use of incomplete information in valuating shares and/or believe that they have accurate information on the future direction of share prices. These beliefs are frequently translated into the mispricing of stocks if the impact of noise traders is not offset by the trading activities of rational investors.

In the case of closed-end funds, they argue that the relative absence of institutional ownership combined with the costs that would be necessary to arbitrage systematic mispricing keeps informed investors out of closed-end fund shares. The authors contend that if noise traders dominate closed-end fund trading, there should be a high correlation among changes in the funds' discounts. The authors identify an initial sample of 87 funds appearing within the 1960-1987 period. Upon investigating the behavior of discounts for nine funds, they find strong evidence of co-movement.

After examining the pattern of new fund offerings and average discounts on seasoned funds, they report evidence consistent with their hypothesis that new funds are offered when discounts shrink to near zero or move to a premium. Additionally, the authors find a strong relation between the returns earned by small firms and the narrowing of discounts on closed-end funds. Like other small firms, closed-end fund share price returns exhibit a "January effect" -- even when changes in the fund's net asset value do not.

They regress changes in closed-end fund discounts against a series of "macro-factors" previously identified by Chen, Roll, and Ross (1986) and find little association. The evidence indicates that discounts on closed-end funds are not a proxy for these fundamental factors. Upon further analysis, they find a negative relation between changes in closed-end fund discounts and the redemption of open-end funds, which they contend supports the small noise trader hypothesis. The authors conclude that closed-end fund discounts provide a strong measure of noise trader sentiment.

De Long, J. Bradford and Andrea Shleifer. "The Stock Market Bubble of 1929: Evidence from Closed-End Funds." *Journal of Economic History* 51.3 (September 1991): 675-700.

De Long and Shleifer reference the sharp run-up and subsequent decline in U.S. stock prices in late 1929 as one of the most striking episodes in U.S. financial market history. Many prior authors conclude that the run-up in prices was ex-ante rational -- that is, based on bullish expectations for the performance of the U.S. economy. The subsequent decline in stock prices was also rational if one believes that investors realized that the performance of the economy would falter.

De Long and Shleifer argue that Lee, et al. (1991) make a convincing case that the discounts on closed-end funds are a measure of noise trader sentiment. If this hypothesis is accepted, the behavior of closed-end fund (CEIC) pricing relative to net asset value (NAV) can be used to help interpret the events of 1929.

They conclude that the run-up in stock prices in 1929 was the result of irrational sentiment because the median closed-end fund premium in late 1929 was approximately 50%. In addition, the authors note the heavy flood of CEIC IPOs during this period, which apparently took advantage of the irrational pricing of both the market and of seasoned closed-end funds. Thirdly, the authors find a strong correlation between changes in the median closed-end fund discount and share price returns during 1929.

In addition to the sentiment arguments, the authors make two other contributions. First, the authors note that when the market began to decline sharply in October of 1929, closed-end funds began reporting the composition of their portfolios. Although likely at first in an effort to convince shareholders that reported NAV reflected current market conditions, the reporting has since become a mandated practice for the entire fund industry. Second, the authors suggest that the flood of closed-end fund IPOs in the late 1920s may have "crowded out" retail and manufacturing issues -- contributing to the softness in the real economy that followed.

De Long, J. Bradford and Andrei Shleifer. "Closed-end fund discounts: A yardstick of small-investor sentiment." *Journal of Portfolio Management* (Winter 1992): 46-53.

The authors argue that the narrowing of discounts on domestic closed-end fund discounts in the mid-1980s, from their prior levels of 15%-20% down to 5%, was responsible for the mid-decade boom in closed-end fund IPOs. This assertion is based on their contention that discounts on closed-end funds are a measure of the sentiment of small investors. When small investors are bullish/bearish on a particular set of financial assets (e.g., stocks), the authors argue that discounts shrink/increase.

They review evidence on the growth of closed-end fund IPOs in the U.S. during the 1920s, and they cite the tremendous premiums at which some closed-end funds traded during the period just prior to the crash. After the crash, the situation reversed and most closed-end funds sold at substantial discounts.

The authors review evidence from the 1980s and pronounce a linkage between the narrowing of discounts and the wave of closed-end fund IPOs. They also argue that the growth in foreign closed-end fund IPOs is to be expected, as many of the early funds' shares were at large premiums over their NAV. The authors close with a quick walk through the rational explanations offered by Malkiel (1977), who addresses discounts. After briefly discussing the issue of premiums, they conclude that discounts/premiums must be an index of small investor sentiment.

Brauer, Greggory A. "Investor Sentiment and the Closed-End Fund Puzzle: A 7 Percent Solution." *Journal of Financial Services Research* (1993): 199-216.

Following the papers summarized above, Brauer attempts to determine the proportion of changes in closed-end fund discounts that can be attributed to noise-traders. The author modifies and applies a technique developed by French and Roll (1986) to estimate the amount of variance in weekly changes in discounts/premiums attributable to the noise trading model developed by De Long, Schleifer, Summers and Waldman (1990).

French and Roll argue that the impact of noise traders is more pronounced in the short run (daily) than in the long run, as errors are ultimately reversible. French and Roll examine the relation between observed six-month return variances and implied six-month return variances from daily data. The authors argue that this noise extraction technique ratio forms a lower boundary for the percentage of variability in daily trading that is attributable to noise-traders.

Brauer estimates a noise extraction ratio from weekly data on a sample of 20 closed-end funds between 1965 and 1990. The results suggest that only about 7% of the variability in closed-end fund discounts can be attributed to the noise traders. In addition, he computes an estimate of the noise extraction ratio for weekly return data on five size-ranked portfolios during similar time periods and finds much higher ratios for small and large firms. Brauer finds no negative relation between extraction ratio measures of noise trader volume and firm size. He concludes that the impact of noise traders is not trivial, but that it is not the driving force behind closed-end fund discounts levels and variability.

Chen, Nai-Fu, Raymond Kan and Merton H. Miller. "Are the Discounts on Closed-End Funds a Sentiment Index?" *Journal of Finance* 48.2 (June 1993): 795-800.

In contrast to the findings of Lee, et al. (1991) (LST), who conclude that discounts on closed-end funds are a measure of noise-trader sentiment, Chen, Kan, and Miller (CKM) find that changes in discounts are highly negatively correlated with the returns on "small" stocks in the 1965-1985 period. CKM note the failure of LST to find consistent evidence of a relation between small firm returns and discounts on closed-end funds.

CKM propose a more direct test of the investor sentiment hypothesis as it relates to small firms. They identify the decile of smallest firms and split this group into those small firms with virtually no institutional ownership (less than 10% of outstanding shares) and those with more institutional ownership. When the returns on the smallest firm sub-samples are regressed against changes in discounts and changes in the value-weighted index of the NYSE (as per LST), the results are statistically identical. CKM contend that this lack of significant difference casts doubt on any association between changes in closed-end fund discounts and returns on small firms.

CKM then regress returns to shareholders of closed-end funds against their contemporaneous changes in net asset value and find an explanatory power of nearly 73%. When the regression is augmented with portfolio returns based on size deciles, the size-based excess return measure is significant for all 10 deciles. However, the gain in explanatory power is small (not more than 4%) and there is nothing unique about the fit obtained with the smallest firm excess return measure. The authors conclude that the evidence refutes the small-firm/closed-end fund discount connection argued by LST and thus critically undermines the investor sentiment hypothesis.

Chopra, Navin, Charles M.C. Lee, Andrei Shleifer, and Richard Thaler.
"Yes, Discounts on Closed-End Funds Are a Sentiment Index."
Journal of Finance 48.2 (June 1993): 801-808.

The authors (CLST) respond to the Chen, et al. (1993) (CKM) claim that the original work by Lee, et al. (1991) tries to kill two birds, the closed-end fund puzzle and the small firm effect, with one stone and misses both. The authors address the critiques raised by CKM.

First, the CKM paper alleges that the smallest firm/closed-end fund discount link reported by Lee, et al. uses a sample that is over-represented by utilities. CLST divide a portfolio of NYSE-listed utilities into three institutional ownership groups and regress the returns against changes in closed-end fund discounts and returns on the value-weighted NYSE. They find the low and medium ownership utility groups are more strongly linked to closed-end fund discounts than is the high ownership portfolio. This finding is robust when the sample period is split in half (1965-75, 1975-85).

Second, these authors argue that the CKM test of sub-samples of utilities created by institutional ownership (more than 10%, less than 10%) does not refute Lee, et al.'s conclusions. CLST point out that CKM's portfolio of "high" institutional ownership really does not have high institutional ownership in an absolute or relative sense. They split each size-ranked decile into three sub-groups based on institutional ownership and re-run the Lee, et al. regressions. They find that within each decile except the first, low institutional ownership firm returns co-move more strongly with discount changes than do medium and high institutional ownership firms.

Third, CSLT restructure a model put forward by CKM that appears to refute Lee, et al. The authors subtract changes in a closed-end fund's NAV from the contemporaneous change in the value of its shares, to produce an excess return. They regress these excess returns against the excess return of size-ranked portfolio returns and find that excess returns on closed-end funds are most strongly related to excess returns earned by the smallest firm portfolios. The authors argue that these finding are consistent with the prior findings and assertions made by Lee, et al.

Chen, Nai-Fu, Raymond Kan, and Merton H. Miller. "A Rejoinder." *Journal of Finance* 48.2, (June 1993): 809-810.
and
Chopra, Navin, Charles M.C. Lee, Andrei Shleifer, and Richard H. Thaler. "Summing Up." *Journal of Finance* 48.23 (June 1993): 811-812.

Chen, Kan and Miller re-stress their original point -- no matter how well refined, excess returns on size-ranked portfolio add only about 4% to our understanding of changes in the discounts on closed-end funds. Chopra, et al. reply that changes in discounts on closed-end funds explain more of the variation in returns on small firms than any of the fundamental factors identified in Chen, Roll, and Ross (1986).

Noronha, Gregory M. and Bruce L. Rubin. "Closed-End Bond Fund Discounts: Agency Costs, Investor Sentiment and Portfolio Content." *Journal of Economics and Finance* 19.3 (Summer, 1995): 29-44.

The authors employ a sample of 24 bond funds between 1980 and 1990 to investigate the factors often posited to influence closed-end fund discounts. The funds sold at a mean discount to NAV in all years except 1985-87. Overall, the average discount was 2.5%, which is substantially smaller than the average discounts reported for equity funds during the same period of time.

Based primarily on the works of Malkiel (1977), Brickley, et al. (1991), Lee, et al. (1991), Kumar and Noronha (1992), and Barclay, et al. (1993), the authors present a five-factor model to explain closed-end bond fund discounts. The factors are: unrealized capital appreciation, restricted securities in the portfolio, large block-holders, management expenses, and investor sentiment. In addition, the authors include a measure of the shape of the yield curve and the spread between bond and stock yields to capture the effect of changing financial market conditions. The authors use the percentage of the fund's portfolio invested in foreign securities, privately placed securities, and junk bonds as proxies for the restricted security factor.

Using a multiple regression model, the authors find strong empirical support for the predicted influence of expense ratios on the closed-end bond fund discounts. In addition, the authors find that increased foreign asset and junk bond holdings increase the size of the bond-fund discounts. No statistical significance is found for the percentage of private placement securities in the fund's portfolio, or the amount of shares controlled by large stockholders. Most problematic is the influence of unrealized capital gains on the size of the discount. The factor is highly significant but its sign is negative; whereas previous theory predicts a positive relation between discounts and unrecognized capital gains. In addition, the authors use a dummy variable to control for years 1985-87. The coefficient estimate for this dummy is negative and highly significant, implying that discounts declined nearly 5% in these three years. The authors argue that this is a result of small investors having an unusual interest in junk bonds, and thus they bid up the price of the closed-end bond funds. They adopt the Lee, et al. explanation that swings in discounts are a manifestation of investor sentiment.

Bodurtha, James N. Jr., Dong-Soon Kim, and Charles M.C. Lee.
"Closed-End Country Funds and U.S. Market Sentiment."
Review of Financial Studies 8.3 (Fall 1995): 879-919.

The authors extend the Lee, et al. (1991) investor sentiment hypothesis to closed-end country funds (CECFs). They observe that CECFs trade in the U.S. market; whereas the fund's net asset value (NAV) is determined in a foreign market. If U.S. investors over- or under-react to information from the foreign market or respond to information that has no intrinsic value, there would be a de-coupling of movements in the CECF share price and its underlying NAV. Put differently, the premium/discount on the CECF should react to domestic forces, and the authors claim that such changes capture the *differential* investor sentiment (domestic vs. foreign market).

The authors examine the contemporaneous correlation in weekly changes in CECF discounts for 33 funds between January 1986 and December 1989. In general, they report that CECFs traded at a premium during the period (domestic CEICs at a discount) and that premiums were largest for Asian funds, while European funds traded on average at a discount. Many pairs of CECFs exhibited substantial contemporaneous correlation in the movement of their premiums/discounts. In addition, changes in the premiums/discounts on CECFs were positively correlated with U.S. market returns; whereas domestic CEICs discount changes were not.

The authors then examine the relation between changes in CECF discounts, share prices, and NAVs to: local market returns, U.S. market returns, and exchange rates. The authors find that CECF discounts changes and CECF returns are positively related to U.S. market returns; whereas changes in CECF NAVs are positively related to local market returns.

As in Lee, et al., the authors examine the relation between U.S. size-ranked portfolio returns and changes in domestic closed-end fund premiums, the U.S. market return, and a third factor: changes in the CECF premiums.

The authors report positive and significant (but monotonically declining) coefficients for two fund premium changes -- consistent with the noise-trader hypothesis and the *differential* investment sentiment hypothesis.

The authors further disaggregate each of the U.S. size-ranked portfolios into three groups, based on institutional ownership (high, medium, low) and find the "domestic" sentiment hypotheses is consistently more robust at the lowest ownership levels. They report that for small firms, the influence is negative -- suggesting that small U.S. stock and CECFs may be gross substitutes for noise-traders.

Finally, the authors examine the ability of CECF premiums to predict future changes in the premiums, future CECF share price returns, and future NAV returns. The authors report that high/low levels of CECF premiums are associated with lower/higher fund share returns -- results consistent with a mean-reversion process that has been previously reported for domestic CEIC trading rules.

Leonard, David C. and David M. Shull. "Investor Sentiment and the Closed-End Fund Evidence: Impact of the January Effect."
The Quarterly Review of Economics and Finance 36.1 (Spring, 1996): 117-126.

The authors seek to resolve the controversy among the above authors over the linkage between changes in closed-end fund (CEIC) discounts and returns to small firm shareholders. Throughout the paper, they discuss issues that could have been responsible for the prior findings.

They employ a sample of 38 closed-end stock funds for the 1965-1994 period. The authors demonstrate that the positive relation between returns to small firms and closed-end fund shareholders is strong between 1965 and 1980, but weak in the period from 1980 to 1994. The authors find that the strong relation in the first half of their sample period is due to returns to both small firms and CEICs in the month of January. They offer that the co-movement may vanish after 1980 because of increased institutional activity in smaller firms. While the authors do not exclude the possibility that investor sentiment drives closed-end fund pricing, they do conclude that tax motivations are important for the individual investors who are the primary holders of closed-end fund shares.

Swaminathan, Bhaskaran. "Time-Varying Expected Small Firm Returns and Closed-End Fund Discounts." *Review of Financial Studies* 9.3 (Fall 1996): 845-887.

Swaminathan undertakes an extensive investigation of the ability of discounts on closed-end funds (CEICs) to explain expected returns on small firm stocks. The author replicates and expands the analysis of Lee, et al. (1991) in investigating the relationship between small firm stocks and CEIC discounts using 33 funds' data for July 1965 through December 1985. The author finds that closed-end fund discounts forecast returns to small firm stockholders. This ability is robust even in the presence of other factors that are employed to model the returns to small firm stockholders.

The author begins the analysis by demonstrating that the long-term stability between excess returns on closed-end fund share prices and NAV are strongly and virtually identically related to changes in dividend growth rates and real interest rates. As a result, the author argues that changes in real interest rates and dividend growth rates are not the driving force of changes in closed-end funds discounts. The author then analyzes changes in CEIC discounts and the relation between closed-end fund discounts and returns to small firm stockholders.

Swaminathan expands the analysis of Lee, et al. in investigating the relationship of closed-end fund (CEIC) discounts and small firm expected returns. Using data for 33 funds for the 1965-1985 period in a long horizon regression framework, the author obtains results indicating that CEIC discounts forecast future excess returns on small firms. The small firm factor is the only factor of the five stock and bond return factors proposed by Fama and French (1993). The other two stock factors (market factor and book-to-market factor) and the two bond factors (default risk factor and term risk factor) are not associated with discounts. Further tests show that discounts forecast future inflation and future earning growth rates.

While the author establishes a linkage between closed-end fund discounts and returns to small firm shareholders consistent with the investor sentiment hypothesis offered by Lee, et al., the other findings do not support the hypothesis. The author concludes that the finding that closed-end fund discounts have some ability to predict real earnings growth (and to a lesser extent, future inflation) does not support the irrationality portion of the sentiment hypothesis.

Pontiff, Jeffrey. "Excess Volatility of Closed-End Funds." *American Economic Review* 87.1, (March 1997): 155-167.

Expanding on the work of Shiller (1990), Pontiff examines the volatility of returns on portfolios held by closed-end funds and the contemporaneous volatility of the returns to shareholders of the funds. Pontiff argues that if closed-end funds were simply a transparent reflection of the underlying portfolio of the fund, the value of the fund's shares and the net asset value (NAV) would behave identically.

Using an identical sample to that of Lee, et al.. (1991), the author first examines the relation between the NAVs of open and closed-end fund NAVs to changes in the CRSP value-weighted index and concludes that they follow similar investment strategies. One cannot reject the hypothesis that they have equal correlation in returns with the market proxy. Pontiff's primary finding is that closed-end fund shares are 64% more volatile than the assets that they own. He reports that only 15% of the average funds' excess volatility is explained by market risk, small firm risk, book-to-market risk, or risk associated with discount movements of other funds.

Pontiff attempts to explain the excess volatility with a variety of factors. The author finds that closed-end funds with large discounts have portfolios that have more stocks with high book-to-market risk than closed-end funds with small discounts. There is some weak evidence that closed-end funds with large discounts have portfolios with smaller average systematic risk measures. However, the author concludes that the efficient market hypothesis is not supported by his findings.

Sias, Richard. "The Sensitivity of Individual and Institutional Investors' Expectations to Changing Market Conditions: Evidence from Closed-End Funds." *Review of Quantitative Finance and Accounting* 8.1 (1997): 245-269.

The author posits that closed-end fund prices can differ from the fund's portfolio net asset value (NAV) due to the existence of "frictions." However, he asserts that variations in discounts could be a result of shifts in shareholder expectations of management performance. Conversely, the author suggests that the variability in discounts could be a result of differences in changes in expectations of the future performance of assets in the portfolio.

Put differently, the owners of assets held by closed-end funds are primarily institutional/large investors; whereas the owners of closed-end fund shares are primarily small investors. If these two groups do not have identical valuation paradigms, there could be systematic differences between the behavior of the fund's portfolio and the fund's shares.

Sias prepares a sample of monthly returns from 54 closed-end funds between July 1965 and December 1990. He relates returns to closed-end fund shareholders, returns on closed-end fund NAVs, and changes in closed-end fund discounts, to six economic variables and three investor sentiment variables. If the heterogeneous valuation hypothesis (small vs. institutional investors) is correct, the sensitivity of the return series should be different across one or more of the explanatory variables.

Sias finds that the six economic factors explain about 12% of the variability in closed-end fund discounts and that the explanatory power doubles when odd-lot trading volume is added to the set of independent variables. Individuals, through the discount, appear to be more sensitive to changes in: consumption growth, the default premium (difference between high- and low-risk bond yields), the yield curve, and unanticipated inflation. The author concludes that the impact of the odd-lot trading volume factor and the differential slope estimates (small vs. large) is consistent with the "over reaction to economic data" hypothesis ascribed to small investors by Lee, et al. (1991) and by De Long, Shleifer, Summers and Waldman (1990).

Sias, Richard. "Price Pressure and the Role of Institutional Investors in Closed-End Funds." *Journal of Financial Research* 20.2 (Summer 1997): 211-229.

The author compiles a data set of closed-end fund (CEIC) share transactions that identifies traders as institutional or individual investors for the November 5, 1990, though January 25, 1991, period. He examines the impact of order-flow imbalance on movements in closed-end fund share prices and on discounts, as well as the role of institutional traders on the market for shares of CEICs. Previously, low net ownership of institutional investors has been used to imply that this group of investors has little influence on the pricing of CEICs. The role of institutional investors is critical to the hypothesis that discounts on closed-end funds are a measure of the sentiment of noise-traders.

Sias tests the price-pressure hypothesis by examining the effect of order-flow imbalance on closed-end fund share prices and on discounts. If price pressure influences closed-end fund share prices and discounts, positive order-flow imbalance (i.e., a preponderance of buy-initiated orders) should increase the share prices and should shrink discounts. The converse should hold.

The author employs the Lee and Ready (1991) method to classify orders as buy- or sell-initiated by examining the relation of the transaction price to the bid/ask prices prior to the sale. If the transaction is at (or near) the ask/bid price, the transaction is classified as "buy-initiated"/"sell initiated." Once classified, the author constructs an index of relative order-flow imbalance for each fund that reflects the cumulative weekly net balance in orders. Returns on closed-end fund shares and changes in the discount are positively related to buy order-imbalance. This holds when contemporaneous changes in NAV are incorporated into the analysis.

Sias identifies control firms with similar market value to each of the closed-end funds. He compares the percent of institutional ownership of the closed-end funds to the control group and finds significantly less ownership for the funds. Sias reports that buyer-initiated institutional volume is dramatically higher for closed-end funds than for the control groups. Institutions are far more actively involved in the market for closed-end funds shares than is evidenced by end-of-quarter measures of ownership.

The author regresses changes in closed-end fund share returns and discounts against the measures of institutional and individual (buyer-induced) order-imbalance and reports that both have positive influences on price and negative influences on discounts. Moreover, Sias finds that the sensitivity measures for institutional and individual order-imbalance are statistically identical.

Finally, Sias finds no support for the hypothesis that the trading behavior of individual investors exposes institutional investors to additional risks. There is no evidence that trends in pricing continue, which would be consistent with the irrational behavior hypothesis ascribed to small investors. The micro-market performance of closed-end fund shares appears to behave as other firms' shares.

Abraham, Abraham, Don Elan, and Alan J. Marcus. "Does Sentiment Explain Closed-End Fund Discounts? Evidence from Bond Funds." *Financial Review* 28.4 (November 1998): 607-619.

Abraham, Elan and Marcus employ a sample of 71 stock and 120 bond closed-end funds (CEICs) from January 1985 through December 1989 to compare the discount behaviors of these two type funds. They find that on average stock, CEICs sell for substantial discounts to their net asset value (NAV), whereas bond funds sell at a small premium to NAV.

The authors assert that the Lee, et al. (1991) sentiment index hypothesis requires a narrowing of discounts as market returns rise. They argue that if changes in noise trader investor sentiment are highly correlated across funds, this should increase the systematic risk for this group of assets. To compensate potential investors for this source of risk, closed-end funds should sell at a discount to their NAV. Hence, if this systematic source of risk to investors is larger for stock funds than bond funds, there should be a higher beta estimate for stock funds than bond funds when one regresses changes in discounts against the return on the market.

The authors' estimates of the relation between changes in fund discounts and rates of return on the market on a fund-by-fund basis are rarely significant. However, with a pooled sample, the authors obtain highly significant but negative slope coefficients for both stock and bond funds. The slope estimates are not statistically different. They argue that the failure to obtain different slope coefficients is inconsistent with the investor sentiment hypothesis. Put differently, finding that the price elasticity of discounts, with respect to changes in the return on the market, is the same for bond and stock funds seems inconsistent with the notion that stock funds are riskier than bond funds.

Neal, Richard and Simon M. Wheatley. "Do Measures of Investor Sentiment Predict Returns?" *Journal of Financial and Quantitative Analysis* 33.4 (December, 1998): 523-547.

The authors examine the ability of three factors often associated with small investor sentiment to predict common stock returns or differential rates of return between large and small firm stocks. The three factors are: the average discount on closed-end funds (CEICs), the ratio of odd-lot sales-to-purchases, and the net redemption of open-end mutual funds. The analysis is conducted over different time periods. As a control, the authors examine the ability of eight other factors to explain differential rates of return between large and small firm stocks.

When examining the predictive power of closed-end fund discounts, the authors use calendar year-end discounts reported by Weisenberger from 1933 to 1993. At year-end, the value-weighted discount for un-levered closed-end domestic stock funds average 12%, ranging from a high of 30% in 1940 to a low of –10% (a premium) in 1969. The authors estimate a number of models, examining the predictive power for the next months; quarters; one-, two-, three- and four-year periods.

For the univariate models employing CEIC discount as the explanatory factor for CRSP returns, the authors find the strongest relation when predicting small firm returns. The year-end discount is statistically significant for small firms, except when predicting first quarter returns. It is never significant when predicting large firm returns. The relation between discounts and small firm returns is positive – as discounts rise, future returns to small firms shareholders increase.

The consistency and strength of these findings are argued to be consistent with the investor sentiment hypothesis. When small investors turn bearish, they sell closed-end fund shares and drive the discount higher. Subsequent return evidence in the overall market proves their timing to be wrong – share prices ultimately rise even when the month of January is excluded. The authors report similar findings for the net redemption factor but not the odd-lot factor.

Brown, Gregory W. "Volatility, Sentiment, and Noise Traders." *Financial Analysts Journal* 55.2, (March/April 1999): 82-90.

The author argues that noise traders are irrational investors acting coherently on a noisy signal and that this can cause systematic risk. If these traders impact asset prices, the risk is manifested in asset return variability. This analysis leads Brown to predict a positive relation between closed-end fund discounts and their volatility. He extends the analysis to predict that this volatility must be at work only when the market is open and that sentiment-driven volatility should be positively related to trading volume.

Brown compiles daily trading data for 1993 and 1994 for a sample of 17 diversified domestic equity closed-end funds (CEFs) and computes a variety of variability measures for each of the funds. In contrast to many earlier studies, the author employs a direct measure of investor sentiment computed from weekly data taken from the *American Association of Individual Investors' Investor Sentiment Survey.*

The author finds a strong positive relation between CEF volatility and changes in both discounts and in market volatility. In addition, he reports that changes in investor sentiment are associated with increases in CEF price volatility. The author finds that sentiment-driven volatility is strong during open-market periods and is virtually nonexistent during closed-market periods. The coefficient on the change in discount variable is significant for closed-market periods, which suggests that discount information is incorporated into prices during this term. In addition, the author finds evidence of a "week-end" effect in CEF trading. Monday trading activity in closed-end funds is elevated beyond what one would expect, given market volatility and changes in discounts. The author concludes that his findings lend support to the Lee, et al. (1991) irrational investor hypothesis.

Chapter 5

CLOSED-END COUNTRY FUNDS AND INTERNATIONAL DIVERSIFICATION BENEFITS

1. INTRODUCTION

At the end of World War II, Japan lay in ruins, her industrial capacity virtually destroyed in the military campaign. With foresight and well-spent financial support, the economy experienced a period of unprecedented growth that catapulted the nation from one of the most destitute to one of the richest on the face of the earth. Given the tremendous success of the Japanese economy, it is frequently not remembered that the recovery process was initially extremely fragile. Early on, in an effort to encourage local business, the Japanese government enacted strict restrictions on imports and on foreign ownership. While many economists argue that the protectionism that dominated the Japanese government's business policy for decades is partly responsible for their current recession, there is little doubt that the policies served their initial purpose.

The booming nature of the Japanese economy drew interest from U.S. and other foreign investors during the late 1950s and early 1960s. Prohibited from direct ownership of equity positions in Japanese firms, these investors were eager to participate in the revitalization of the economy. In response to investor interest, the first modern closed-end "country fund" was created -- the Japan Fund.

The Japan Fund, listed on the New York Stock Exchange, was the darling of Wall Street during the mid-1960s and 1970s. It offered the only avenue for U.S. investors to participate in the growth of the Japanese economy. Not surprisingly, the fund frequently traded at a large premium to its net asset value (NAV). However, as restrictions against foreign ownership of shares in Japanese firms decreased, so did the premium of the fund. Ultimately the fund was converted into an open-end fund in 1987, with little fanfare.

The Japan Fund typified the potential gains and risks faced by those who invest in closed-end country funds. When a fund represents virtually the only way foreign investors can participate in the country's financial markets, the fund usually trades at a premium to its underlying value. However, this premium is an artifact of political policies, which can change.

No matter how interesting, finance articles rarely limit themselves to an analysis of an individual firm like the Japan Fund. The literature in this area primarily focuses on the ability of closed-end country funds to deliver diversification benefits relative to the benefits from investing in the funds' underlying securities. Several studies find that fund returns do not mirror returns of their target market's index, and the analyses are generally expanded to determine what factors are responsible for this finding.

It took the widespread development of closed-end country funds to provide the breadth of observations needed to encourage empirical analysis. However, the interest in foreign investments by closed-end funds researchers predates this literature. Several early cross-sectional models of closed-end fund discounts include the existence of foreign securities in their general discussion of "restricted securities" which do not trade on open markets. Those models often posit a negative relation between closed-end fund discounts and restricted shares, whereas most current researchers view foreign investments as having a potentially positive influence on the fund's discount. Thus, some of the early cross-sectional models may be biased in their findings by having combined two empirical factors into one measure (e.g., the percentage of the fund's portfolio invested in restricted and foreign securities).

Bosner-Neal, Catherine, Greggory Brauer, Robert Neal, and Simon Wheatley. "International Restrictions and Closed-End Country Fund Prices." *Journal of Finance* 45.2 (June 1990): 523-547.

Many countries, including the United States, impose restrictions on the real and portfolio investment activities of non-residents. To the extent that these restrictions are binding, they serve to segment the local capital market, making the price of risk a function of where capital is raised. The economics and finance literature contains many tests of the capital market integration or segmentation hypothesis.

Bosner-Neal, et al. offer a method to determine if restrictions are binding via an investigation of the premiums/discounts on closed-end country funds (CECFs). The authors argue that if restrictions are binding, foreign investors pay a premium over net asset value (NAV) for the shares of a CECF specializing in the segmented market. If capital markets restrictions are subsequently loosened/tightened, the authors predict that the CECF premium will decline/increase.

The authors employ a sample of 33 domestic (U.S.) closed-end funds to serve as a control group and examine the behavior of weekly returns of 14 CECFs between May 1981 and January 1989. On average, the CECFs exhibit substantially smaller discounts during the sample period than the domestic control group (4.5% vs. 11.2%).

The authors identify changes in international investment restrictions through a search of the *Wall Street Journal Index* and the International Monetary Fund's *Exchange Arrangements and Exchange Restrictions*. They. regress changes in CECF discounts against three dummy variables, with an intercept coefficient. The first and third dummy variables take on 1 (-1) (loosening and tightening, respectively) in event weeks (-2 through -7) and (2 through 7), respectively, while the second dummy variable takes on the value 1 (-1) in event weeks (-1, 0, 1), where 0 represents the week of the change in the restriction. Regression coefficients during the three-week event period (-1, 0, 1) are negative and highly significant -- a loosening/tightening of restrictions leads to a decline/increase in the CECF premium.

They find that four of the five country funds examined display a significant decrease in price-to-NAV ratios in anticipation of, or after the announcement of, investment restriction liberalization. They conclude that government-imposed barriers have been effective in segmenting asset markets. Thus, the cost of capital depends on the country of origination.

Bailey, Warren and Joseph Lim. "Evaluating the Diversification of New Country Funds." *Journal of Portfolio Management* (Spring 1992): 74-80.

The authors examine the proposition that shareholders of closed-end funds specializing in foreign investments (CECFs) reap the international diversification benefits thought to be gained by direct portfolio investments in these economies. In some cases, closed-end funds provide the only mechanism by which a U.S. investor can gain access to the foreign market, albeit indirectly.

The authors find CECF share returns to be strongly correlated with U.S. market returns. Conversely, the authors find substantially lower contemporaneous correlation between the target country market index and the U.S. market index. This suggests that the returns to CECF shareholders are determined more by U.S. than by target market conditions.

The authors also estimate an efficient frontier using the U.S. market index augmented by the CECF shares and re-estimate the frontier using the U.S. and foreign market indices. Given the influence of the U.S. market on the CECF returns, it is not surprising that the frontier employing underlying assets dominates the frontier employing CECFs. However, the frontier with the CECFs dominates the U.S. market-only result. These results suggest that international diversification is beneficial, but that CECFs are a poor vehicle for delivering those benefits.

In addition, the authors examine the volatility of returns to CECFs during trading hours in New York and during non-trading hours (i.e., the difference between the closing price and the following opening price). Since many of the CECFs invest in markets that are closed when trading takes place in New York (or the overlap is minimal), one might expect the volatility of CECF returns to be highest when the market is closed. However, in most of the cases examined, this is not the case.

Johnson, Gordon, Thomas Schneeweis and William Dinning. "Closed-End Country Funds: Exchange Rate and Investment Risk."
Financial Analysts Journal (November/December 1993): 74-82.

The authors examine four different risk-return issues for closed-end country funds (CFs). Using monthly data from 1989 through 1992 for a sample of 14 funds targeting 13 different countries, the authors develop a number of sample statistics for "raw" and "hedged" returns for the funds' share price, the funds' net asset value (NAV), and the local market indices. The results demonstrate that, from a U.S. (dollar-hedged) perspective, developed markets experience significantly less exchange rate volatility than do emerging markets. For the developed markets, returns during the period were highly correlated with U.S. returns; whereas many emerging markets' returns were independent of U.S. returns.

The lack of a strong correlation between U.S. returns and emerging market returns promises the possibility of significant diversification benefits for U.S. investors. To determine whether the CFs can deliver these benefits, the authors regress share price returns and NAV returns against local and U.S. market returns in a two-factor model. The authors report a strong relation between emerging market CF share price returns and the U.S. market (while the influence on NAV returns is much less). The relation between developed market CF share price returns and the U.S. market is not as strong.

The authors posit that their evidence supports the hypothesis that noise-trader sentiment explains a sizable portion of closed-end fund discounts. Noise-traders are usually small investors who irrationally act on limited information (e.g., price movements) and who may cause CF share prices (especially emerging market funds) to behave irrationally.

The authors examine the role of currency hedging in the evaluation of CF shares and find that complete hedging during this period actually increases the total variability of dollar denominated returns. Changes in local currency values during the sample period are slightly negatively correlated with returns on the CF shares and their NAV. By allowing the currency risk to go un-hedged, the overall variability of these investments is reduced, from a U.S. point-of-view.

Finally, the authors re-examine the ability of CFs to provide U.S. investors with reduced risk in the context of a total portfolio comprising U.S. investments and CF investments. When split 75% (U.S.) / 25% (CF), the variability in portfolio returns declines (relative to 100% U.S.). This holds when the foreign component is either the fund's NAV or the local market. However, no decline in variability occurs when the foreign component is CF shares. As vehicles for delivering diversification benefits, CFs are easier than direct investments, especially in emerging markets, but they are not perfect substitutes.

Chowdhury, Abdur R. "The Behavior of Closed-End Country Fund Prices in the Asian NIEs." *Applied Economic Letters* 1 (1994): 219-222.

Prior analyses of the premiums/discounts that often characterize closed-end country funds (CECFs) report evidence consistent with the hypothesis that investment restrictions on foreign investors lead to premiums. In addition, prior research demonstrates that when an economy relaxes restrictions on foreign investment, the amount of the premium declines for CECFs. This paper re-examines these hypotheses through analysis of CECFs that target four newly industrialized economies (NIEs) in Asia: Hong Kong, Korea, Singapore, and Taiwan.

In all four instances, the government in question relaxes restrictions on foreign investors. In two cases, Hong Kong and Singapore, the economies have highly developed financial markets before the restrictions on investments are relaxed. Conversely, Korea and Taiwan have relatively undeveloped financial markets at the time the restrictions are relaxed.

For both Korea and Taiwan the decrease in investment restrictions is accompanied by large and statistically significant declines in CECF premiums. Conversely, the decrease in investment restrictions in Singapore and Hong Kong have no statistically significant impact on their respective closed-end country fund premiums. As a result, the author concludes that changes in premiums associated with changes in foreign investor restrictions are conditional upon the extent of restrictions on foreign investment at the time of the change in policy.

Medewitz, Jeanette N., Fuad A. Adullah, and Keith Olson.
"An Investigation Into the Market Valuation Process of Closed-End Country Funds." *FM Letters* (Spring 1994): 13-14.

In this short write-up, the authors report that changes in country fund (CF) share price and changes in their net asset value (NAV) are driven by changes in their local market index, when the country's capital markets are well established. However, changes in the S&P 500 explain changes in the Korean, Philippines, Singapore, and Thailand Funds' share price and NAV; while changes in their respective local markets index prove insignificant. The authors also report that the ratio of fund share price to NAV (greater than 1 indicates a premium) is better explained by variations in a fund's share price than by variations in its NAV.

Chang, Eric, Cheol S. Eun, Richard Kolodny. "International diversification through closed-end country funds." *Journal of Banking and Finance* 19.4 (1995): 1237-1263.

The authors examine the weekly returns of a sample of 15 closed-end country funds (CECFs) from January 1985 through December 1990. They find that returns to fund's shareholders exhibit a surprisingly strong correlation with U.S. market returns, but usually (10 of 15 funds) have a stronger correlation with their respective local market.

The authors use a two-factor (U.S. market return and local market return) model to explain returns to shareholders and changes in net asset value (NAV). They find that 12 of the 15 funds' returns to shareholders have significantly higher U.S. market return "betas" than do their respective NAV returns.

Focusing on the returns to CECF shareholders, the authors find they exhibit far greater pair-wise correlation than the correlation in changes in their respective NAVs or local market indices. They report that the average return in this period is above the U.S. market but is substantially more volatile than U.S. returns. When estimating efficient frontiers, the portfolios include many of the CECF shares, but the frontiers obtained using changes in NAVs dominate these results (i.e., higher returns for each level of risk). Thus, while the funds can provide diversification benefits, there is slippage.

Chang, et al., compute a variety of standard performance measures (e.g., Jensen's alpha) and find that only the Mexico Fund delivers positive abnormal performance during the period. Combined with the evidence above, the authors conclude that the gains to U.S. investors for holding CECF come strictly from the diversification benefits.

The authors close with an examination of the relation between changes in the CECF share price and NAV. If the two series are co-integrated, there is little opportunity for arbitrage between the two markets (shares trading in the U.S. while the assets trade in the local market). They reject the co-integration hypothesis in seven of the 15 cases. Further analysis suggests that the markets of the emerging economies of Asia, Brazil, and Spain, are segmented from U.S. capital markets.

Choi, Jongmoo Jay and Insup Lee. "Market Segmentation and the Valuation of Closed-End Country Funds." *Review of Quantitative Finance and Accounting* 7.1 (1996): 45-63.

The authors examine the pricing of closed-end country funds (CECFs) in an effort to gain evidence on the existence of international financial market segmentation. They argue that prices of single country CECFs that trade in the United States would be expected to show some dependency on U.S. market returns and on target market returns. Of interest is whether dependencies translate into these "risks" being priced. If the target market risk factor is priced, the evidence would be consistent with a market-segmentation hypothesis.

Choi and Lee note that most examinations of domestic closed-end fund discounts attempt to model these discounts. However, in the case of CECFs, most trade at premiums. This difference is ad hoc evidence of market segmentation. They argue that premiums arise because governments restrict foreign investor access to local capital markets.

They analyze weekly returns from 1978 through 1990 for a sample of 21 CECFs and find that 5 of the funds have statistically significant discounts over the entire period, while 11 have significant premiums. The authors employ a 0, 1, 2 metric to measure the extent of foreign investor restrictions in a given country. They regress weekly CECF returns against weekly U.S. market returns. In addition, they estimate a three-factor model containing a market segmentation "dummy."

Using a two-step technique, the authors estimate "betas" for their two- and three-factor models and find strong support for both market and segmentation factors. In addition, the authors adopt a method employed by Gibbons (1982) that simultaneously estimates "betas" and the price of risk.

These second models suggest that only the local market factor is priced. When the segmentation dummy factor is included, the pricing of the local market factor is reduced. This evidence is consistent with a market segmentation hypothesis, but only when the local market has significant barriers to foreign investors.

The authors investigate the relation between CECF returns and changes in the value of the target market's currency, finding statistical significance for only four funds. They also estimate a cross-sectional model of CECF discounts (premiums) and find some evidence in support of a currency value effect, but no support for a growth rate, the segmentation dummy, or the capitalization rate effect.

Beckaert, Geert and Michael S. Urias. "Diversification, Integration and Emerging Market Closed-End Funds." *Journal of Finance* 51.3 (July 1996): 835-869.

The authors mount an ambitious study of the diversification benefits to U.S. investors with a sample of 80 closed-end funds, 42 of which specialize in emerging capital market investments (EMCFs) with the remainder investing in developed/mature markets. Forty-three of the funds' shares trade in the U.S.; while the remainder trade in the U.K. The authors report a variety of sample statistics from return data for the period January 1986 through August 1993. They report a 0.92% mean EMCF premium for U.S.-traded funds and -9.51% (i.e., discount) for U.K.-traded funds. The mean premium reported for U.S. and U.K. funds investing in mature markets is -7.09% and -13.06%, respectively. The mean for U.S. and U.K.-based "domestic" funds during the period was -8.25% and -14.64%.

Utilizing a series of mean-variance spanning tests, the authors conclude that the U.S. investor's efficient frontier computed with mature market indices shifts with the inclusion of U.K.-traded EMCFs. However, the U.S. investor's efficient frontier does not shift with the inclusion of U.S-traded EMCFs.

They examine the impact of liberalizing entry of foreigners into the capital markets of Brazil, India, Taiwan, and Korea. As an indirect test of whether the restrictions bind, they investigate whether these changes produce significant difference in the spanning properties of these funds. In the case of Brazil and India the restrictions are not binding before or after the change. For Taiwan the constraint is binding before the change but not after. The result is reversed for Korea (a counter-intuitive result). Thus, Brazil and India offer U.S. investors no special diversification benefits during the period. However, Taiwan offers benefits before liberalizing their capital markets, but not afterward. They report that Korea offers no benefits when their markets are restricted, but do after they are opened during the period of concern.

The authors also conduct a series of tests on the abnormal performance of pairs of U.S. and U.K. funds that invest in the same emerging market. In most cases, the U.K. fund outperforms the U.S. competitor, although the majority of U.K. and U.S. funds fail to exhibit abnormal returns. The cause of the comparative advantage is unclear. It could be because of the portfolio selections of the managers, or it could be due to differences in the behavior of the premiums for the U.S. and U.K. funds.

Arshanapalli, Bala, Jongmo Jay Choi, E. Tyler Clagget, Jr., John Doukas, and Insup Lee. "Explaining Premiums and Discounts on Closed-End Equity Country Funds." *Journal of Applied Corporate Finance* 9.3 (Fall, 1996): 109-117.

This paper investigates the cross-sectional variation exhibited by closed-end country funds. The authors examine the return performance of 28 country funds from 1978 (or their inception) until 1995 and how these returns are correlated with returns on their own country's stock market index and with U.S. stock market returns.

In general, the authors report low correlation in returns between the local countries' stock market index and the U.S. stock market, and that the correlations are generally highest for "developed" markets – but none have a coefficient that exceeds 0.5. These findings suggest that U.S. investors could experience significant reductions in the variability of the value of their total wealth if they engage in foreign portfolio investments.

The authors report that the correlation between returns to the shareholders of the country funds and the U.S. stock market is also low, and in 12 of the 28 cases the returns are lower than the correlation between the local market index and the U.S. stock market. This finding suggests that the closed-end fund may offer even greater diversification gains than are promised by the local market's index. This is primarily due to the low correlation between the local market's return and the return on the closed-end country fund. None of the country funds can be characterized as an index fund.

Moving on to an examination of the discounts/premiums commanded by the country funds, the authors report that a large majority sells at an average discount. The discounts tend to be the largest for the funds that restrict their investments in "developed" markets (France, Germany, and the UK). Conversely, of the eight funds that sell at an average premium, six are associated with local markets that have substantial restrictions on foreign investment.

Using a two-factor model of weekly returns to stockholders of country funds, the authors find strong evidence of a local market influence and surprising strong evidence of a U.S. market influence (significant in 26 of 28 cases). In addition, the authors examine the relation between exchange rate fluctuations and country fund returns, and exchange rate fluctuations and local market index returns. The authors find only weak correlation in 2 of the 28 country funds and exchange rates, and only 5 significant results between the 22 markets and exchange rates.

Errunza, Vihang, Lemma Senbet, and Ked Hogan. "The Pricing of Country Funds from Emerging Markets: Theory and Evidence." *International Journal of Theoretical and Applied Finance* 1.1 (1998): 111-143.

The authors argue that without restrictions on capital flows, arbitrage activities should equalize returns for bearing systematic risk across national borders. In the presence of restrictions/frictions, the return to investors in segmented markets will differ from the predictions of the no-arbitrage model. This difference in returns is argued to be a result of the size of the restrictions and of the extent to which the return-generating factors in the local market are spanned by securities available in developed capital markets. The authors demonstrate these results through construction of an APT-like asset model.

In markets with highly restricted access (usually emerging economies) to foreign investors, one might expect a higher return to investors and conversely, a higher cost of funds to issuers. In local markets that are driven by factors not easily spanned by the securities available to foreign investors, the return to investors should be higher. Alternately, if foreign investors can find substitutes for the performance of the local market, the return "premium" for local shares should be minimized.

Closed-end funds offer foreign investors the prospect of being able to participate in local markets from which they are partially or fully restricted. As a result, the closed-end fund can enhance the efficiency of local markets in two ways. First, the fund encourages foreign capital flows that help to increase pricing efficiency in the local market. Second, the capital flow reduces segmentation, thus reducing capital costs to local firms and reducing returns to foreign shareholders.

With a sample of 32 closed-end country funds, the authors examine the behavior of returns in 1993 and estimate a multi-factor model of fund discounts consistent with their theoretical model. The sample contains 19 "emerging" economy funds and 13 country funds from "developed" markets. Consistent with other studies, the authors find that the country funds fail to perfectly mimic their target market stock index. This finding holds for both "developed" and "emerging" market funds. The authors report that a lack of strong U.S. market influence holds for both developed and emerging market funds. Conversely, the correlation in country fund returns with a "global market" factor is pronounced and holds, even controlling for the influence of U.S. and domestic markets.

The authors report two sets of regression estimates obtained from a cross-sectional model of country fund premiums: one with emerging economy funds and one with developed economy funds. For the 19 emerging economy funds, the authors find that the global factor has the most explanatory power (significant for 16 of the 19 funds), with investor access very important (10 of 19 funds). The lack of easy substitution and the lack of locally available spanning securities have little explanatory power for the premiums on emerging country funds.

For the 13 developed economy funds, the authors also find the global factor most important in explaining discounts, but in a smaller percentage of the funds (8 out of 13). Substitution and spanning factors have virtually no explanatory power, and lack of access is not a factor by definition. Although the empirical evidence is limited to a single calendar year, the results yield evidence that country funds are imperfect vehicles for gaining international investment benefits, as measured by national indexes.

Kramer, Charles and R. Todd Smith. "The Mexican Crisis and the Behavior of Country Fund Discounts: Renewing the Puzzle of Closed-End Fund Pricing." *International Journal of Theoretical and Applied Finance* 1.1 (1998): 164-171.

The authors address the investor sentiment hypothesis posited by Lee, et al. (1990) (LST) and apply it to the behavior of closed-end country funds specializing in Mexican investments. Around the time of the peso crisis in 1994, they contend that one would expect funds to sell at large discounts to net asset value (NAV) – especially after the collapse. Instead, the authors find that in the five months prior to the collapse, the four Mexican funds sell at modest discounts of 3%-5%. At the collapse of the peso, the four Mexican funds begin to sell at premiums. Immediately after the collapse of the peso, the funds sell at premiums as high as 60%.

The authors explain that on the surface, the "cause" of the large premiums for the four Mexican funds is rather simple – the NAVs of the funds collapsed far more rapidly than the funds' prices in the United States. The collapse in NAVs is in part due to the collapse of the peso, which is used to convert peso asset values into dollar asset values, and in part due to the decline in Mexican security prices, which are quoted in pesos.

The authors then examine the impact of the peso crisis on the discounts/premiums of other country funds. They report that other Latin American funds' discounts shrink during the peso crisis. Conversely, the discounts on Asian funds remain virtually unchanged during the peso crisis, while discounts on "developed" market closed-end funds (Germany, Switzerland) are steady or increasing over this time.

In short, there is no evidence of a contagion impact of the peso crisis on closed-end fund discounts. However, weakness in the NAVs of several funds outside of Mexico is associated with the peso crisis. Much of that weakness is attributable to declines in currency values as opposed to market prices for the funds. The authors argue that these findings are inconsistent with the investor sentiment hypothesis espoused by LST. They argue that the evidence is more consistent with a loss-aversion hypothesis; that is, the disutility from a loss is more than the utility increase from an equal size gain.

Ghose, Subrata and Jeffery A. Born. "Asian and Latin American Emerging Market Closed-End Funds: Return and Diversification." *Emerging Markets Quarterly* 2.2 (Fall 1998): 63-75.

Ghose and Born examine the return and risk characteristics of emerging market closed-end funds (EMCFs) investing in Asian and Latin American markets from January 1990 through March 1996. The authors attempt to determine if these markets and/or the funds that invest in them offer return and/or diversification benefits to U.S. investors. Although most Asian and Latin American markets have low average returns during the sample period, the returns are weakly correlated with the U.S. market during the period, suggesting possible diversification benefits.

The authors find the net asset values (NAVs) of the Asian funds to be virtually flat during the period, while the NAVs of Latin American funds increase. The average weekly return to EMCF shareholders is only 0.014% (0.72% yearly). However, like the underlying local markets, the returns on the EMCFs exhibit a low correlation with U.S. market returns, suggesting the possibility of diversification benefits.

In an effort to determine how "transparent" the EMCFs are, the authors examine how closely changes in the fund's NAV and its share price mirror changes in the local market index. Only six of the 51 funds have NAV "local market betas" greater than one, but the explanatory power of the single-factor model is high. Only four have share price local market betas greater than one, and the correlation and explanatory power are low.

Slightly more than half of the funds have share price local market betas greater than their NAV local market betas. Hence, claims of aggressive management are not supported by the data.

Finally, the authors employ a two-factor model (the U.S. market and the target market) to examine the return to EMCF shareholders. They report the explanatory power of the model to be twice that obtained with only the target market factor. The U.S. market factor is statistically significant for 21 of the funds.

The authors stress that during this time period the Asian and Latin American markets' returns are low, and the U.S. market returns are high. They conclude that the low correlation between U.S. market returns and foreign market returns could make investments in these markets attractive for diversification reasons. However, EMCFs appear to be poor vehicles for delivering this benefit.

LaBarge, Karin P. and Richard A. LaBarge. "Portfolio Sets for Latin American Closed-End Country Funds in the Changing Interest Rate Environments of 1992-1994. "*The Journal of Financial Engineering* 5.1 (1996): 37-52.

The authors estimate a series of mean-variance (MV) efficient portfolios employing a sample including the S&P 500 index, U.S. T-bills (a risk-free proxy), and seven closed-end country funds that limit their investments to Latin America. They compare the composition of MV efficient portfolios estimated from return data drawn from a "stable U.S. interest rate" environment (5/92 through 1/94) to the composition of MV efficient portfolios estimated from a "rising U.S. interest rate" environment (2/94 through 11/94). The variation in the composition of ex-post MV efficient portfolios suggests that active investment management may impart value for U.S. investors wishing to obtain a presence in Latin America.

Holding the Sharpe-ratio constants in each sub-period, the authors estimate the proportion of wealth that should be invested in each of the nine candidates. The authors do not permit short sales, thereby constraining portfolio weights to zero or more. They estimate the ex-post composition of portfolios that lie along the MV efficient frontier (in the absence of a risk-free asset) in each sub-period. In both exercises, an infinite number of portfolios can be estimated. Thus, the authors report only a small number of points from each case.

Holding the Sharpe-ratio constant in the stable-rate environment, T-bills gradually replace investments in the S&P 500 and the Mexico Fund. At the limit, the composition is 28.7% in the S&P 500 and 71.3% in the Mexico

Fund. The monthly return dominates the S&P 500 by a large margin (2.6% vs. 0.6%), but it is substantially more volatile. In the rising rate environment, T-bills gradually replace the Brazil Fund. When examining the composition of MV efficient frontier portfolios (allowing weights to vary by 1/8ths), the authors find the same "instability" across the two interest rate environments.

The authors conclude that the instability in the composition of MV efficient portfolios and in the MV efficient frontier make any asset allocation strategy based on historic data problematic. It is highly unlikely that such a strategy would lead to the creation of a portfolio that would lie near the efficient frontier in a subsequent period. The authors argue that this suggests a role for fundamental analysis and active management in order to obtain proper compensation for bearing risk when Latin American assets are included in a selection set by U.S. investors.

Anderson, Seth C., Jay Coleman, Jeff Steagall, and Cheryl Frohlich. "A Multi-Factor Analysis of Country Fund Returns." *Journal of Financial Research* 24.3 (Fall 2001): 331-346.

This paper re-examines the returns to shareholders of closed-end country funds (CECFs) in an effort to determine the underlying influence of the U.S. market. Prior research on CECFs concludes that returns to shareholders are significantly related to U.S. market returns. As a result, much prior research concludes that CECFs fail to deliver the benefits from international diversification that the target market returns would possibly offer.

The authors provide an expanded version of the return-generating process for CECFs, including the target market, exchange rates, discounts/premiums, the U.S. market, and other country markets. They employ weekly data from 34 CECFs for the 222-week period from October 2, 1992, through December 27, 1996. They exclude observations from the time period around the Mexican peso crisis in late 1994.

When returns to shareholders of the CECFs are analyzed, the authors find strong evidence of the influence of local market returns and changes in the fund discounts. For some funds, there is evidence of an exchange rate influence on returns. Only for the UK and Brazil funds do the authors find a strong influence for the U.S. market return, although they find a statistically significant impact on the returns to the shareholders of three other funds.

When the authors augment their four main factors with returns on the other local markets represented in the study, they find some evidence of co-movement. For example, returns to shareholders of the Brazil and Brazil Equity funds are positively related to changes in the Chile market return, and negatively related to changes in the Korean and Spanish market return. There are some cases where the inter-dependence seems to be explained by geographic location (e.g., Brazil, Chile) and others that seem best explained by substitution effects (e.g., Brazil, Korea).

The authors contend that the influence of U.S. market returns on returns to shareholders of CECFs is often overstated because prior authors specify a return-generating process without enough factors. They conclude that CECF returns are not so dominated by the U.S. market conditions as previous research suggests.

Chapter 6

OTHER EFFORTS TO EXPLAIN CLOSED-END FUND DISCOUNTS

1. INTRODUCTION

The two prior chapters dealt with papers addressing issues involving investor sentiment and international funds, two areas that evolved primarily in the 1990s. In this chapter we focus on papers that address rational explanations for CEIC discounts. Some works re-address themes of pre-1990 papers; while others delve into new areas. In these papers, the most popular areas of inquiry are: (A) managerial fees and expenses, (B) tax-timing options, (C) performance management issues, and (D) the ownership position of the fund's managers. Papers in the latter two sub-categories break new ground in thought-provoking ways and appear to represent areas that may spawn future research.

Brickley, James, Steven Manaster, and James Schallheim.
"The Tax-Timing Option and the Discounts on Closed-End Investment Companies." *Journal of Business* 64.3 (1991): 287-312.

The authors build on two earlier papers by Constantinidies (1983, 1984) that argue that taxes have demonstrable influences on asset prices. When individuals purchase taxable securities, they obtain the "option" to sell those securities, recognizing a gain or loss, at their discretion. One would expect investors to time the sale of securities in such a way so as to minimize their expected tax liability. Constantinidies demonstrates that the value of the tax-timing option is positively related to the price variability of the asset's pre-tax rate of return. Put differently, the greater the potential range of security values, the more valuable the security is in a tax-minimization strategy.

Brickley, Manaster, and Schallheim extend this insight into the pricing of closed-end funds. When individuals purchase shares in a fund (open or closed), as opposed to replicating the underlying portfolio of the fund, they forfeit the tax-timing options on the underlying assets to the fund's management, but they gain a tax-timing option on the fund's shares. Whether the individual suffers a net gain or loss from this swap is argued to be a function of the fund's share price variability versus the fund's NAV price variability.

The authors explain that to exploit the value of tax-timing, individuals must engage in transactions and thus bear transactions costs. They argue that the net benefit of a tax-timing option declines as the variability of the individual asset declines. Using data from 1969 through 1978 for funds that have limited investments in restricted securities (< 3% of total portfolio), the authors find a positive relation between discounts and the variability of net asset value returns as predicted by the extended model of Constantinidies. Their findings are also consistent with the investor sentiment hypothesis if investors are "over-optimistic" during expansions and "over-pessimistic" during contractions. However, the investor sentiment hypothesis cannot explain the rational degree of correlation between unrecognized portfolio gains/losses and closed-end fund discounts.

Kumar, Raman, and Gregory M. Noronha. "A Re-Examination of the Relationship Between Closed-End Fund Discounts and Expenses." *Journal of Financial Research* 15.2 (Summer 1992): 139-147.

Malkiel (1977) first offers the hypothesis that closed-end fund discounts are a function of the fund's management expense. In his empirical test, Malkiel defines the expense variable as the management fee divided by the fund's net asset value (NAV). When combined with other variables designed to control for unrecognized capital gains and the percentage of the fund's assets invested in restricted stock, Malkiel finds little support for the management expense hypothesis.

Kumar and Noronha update the Malkiel study, employing a different measure of management fees and adding a variable to control for the percentage of NAV invested in foreign securities. The authors state that management fees are generally determined by a fixed schedule as a percentage of total assets. Thus, as the fund's size increases, management fees rise, but at a slower rate than the growth of fund size. The authors suggest that the non-linear relation between management fees and fund size as proxied by NAV could bias Malkiel's results.

They contend that the value of a financial asset is equal to the discounted value of the expected cash flow distribution to its owner. Because management fees reduce the level of dividends paid to the fund's shareholders, it follows that the value of the fund's shares should be less than its NAV. Thus, they express management fees as a percentage of the fund's gross investment income, of which funds must distribute as dividends in order to maintain tax-exempt status.

The authors examine annual data from 1976 through 1987 with separate models; one using their management fee variable and the other using the management fee variable as defined by Malkiel. In addition, the authors include variables that measure unrecognized capital gains, the percentage of assets invested in restricted stock, and the percentage of assets invested in foreign stock. The overall explanatory power of Kumar and Noronha's model exceeds the power of Malkiel's model.

From the empirical evidence, the authors conclude that differences in management fees do explain a small proportion of the cross-sectional variance in closed-end fund discounts. However, they state that the overall explanatory power of their models is low and posit that other explanatory variables are likely to exist.

Barclay, Michael J., Clifford G. Holderness, and Jeffrey Pontiff. "Private Benefits from Block Ownership and Discounts on Closed-End Funds." *Journal of Financial Economics* 33, (1993): 263-291.

The authors begin with a brief discussion of why closed-end funds are rarely converted to open-end status. They cite prior works by Thompson (1978) and Brauer (1984), who offer that closed-end fund managers might resist the opening of a closed-end fund because it could lead to their replacement as fund managers. This is especially so if the managers have small ownership positions in the fund. Bradley, Holderness, and Pontiff, argue that as managerial ownership increases, the likelihood of a takeover and/or opening the fund increases, and the discount on the fund's shares should decrease.

The authors examine a sample of closed-end stock and bond funds in three different years: 1979, 1984 and 1989. They find that funds with management teams having substantial block ownership positions sell at an average discount of 14.2%; whereas those without large managerial ownership positions have an average discount of 4.1%. In a cross-sectional regression where the discount is the dependent variable, the authors find evidence that "hostile to the management team" block ownership tends to reduce the average discounts by about 40 basis points.

This evidence is in direct opposition to the arguments above. They suggest the analysis fails because as managerial ownership increases, so does their ability to extract resources from the fund 's shareholders. The authors document a number of private business arrangements between closed-end funds and their managers (which in and of itself is fascinating reading). They point out that shareholders of closed-end funds have a limited ability to discipline the offending managers.

Kim, Chang-Soo. "Investor Tax-Trading Opportunities and Discounts on Closed-End Mutual Funds." *Journal of Financial Research* 17.1 (Spring 1994): 65-75.

The author posits that arbitrage activities should induce parity between the net asset value (NAV) per share of a closed-end fund and the market price of its shares. He observes that deviations from parity are pronounced and long-lasting, which has made closed-end funds the subject of much speculation and research. Kim argues that a portion of the discount can be explained by the loss of tax timing opportunities suffered by the investor who purchases shares of a closed-end fund instead of purchasing the fund's portfolio of assets. Thus, the size of the fund's share price discount to its NAV is positively related to the value of the option.

Kim applies Merton's (1976) option pricing theorem to the tax-timing difference between owning the fund's shares and the underlying portfolio. He explains that the value of the tax-trading option is positively related to the return variability of the fund's assets returns and to the number of assets in the fund. Kim demonstrates the sensitivity of the tax-trading option value (discount) to changes in key parameters, and calculates that its theoretical values can be greater than 7% of the value of the portfolio.

Although he does not estimate the value of any tax-trading options for any actual closed-end fund, Kim argues that there is much market and fund data that is consistent with the model. He contends that both the evaporation of discounts for closed-end funds announcing that they are going to open up, and the fact that most closed-end funds that have opened up have been broadly diversified funds, are consistent with his model.

Malkiel, Burton G. "The Structure of Closed-End Fund Discounts Revisited." *Journal of Portfolio Management* (Summer 1995): 32-38.

Malkiel updates his 1977 landmark study in an effort to determine if the previous persistence in closed-end fund discounts continues and whether there are rational explanations for the pattern of discounts observed. Malkiel begins with a re-examination of some of the factors that he originally offered to explain discounts. He then augments these factors with a set of new factors.

Malkiel argues for a positive relation between a closed-end fund's discount and its: unrecognized capital gains, investments in restricted shares of stock, portfolio turnover, payout policy, percentage of the fund's shares held by insiders, and proportion of assets invested in foreign assets. Malkiel argues for an inverse relation between the fund's discount and both its size and its historical rate of return. He utilizes a sample of 30 funds to test these hypotheses.

In a series of univariate regressions, Malkiel finds support for the restricted stock and unrecognized capital gains hypothesis. Although he finds portfolio turnover is positively related to premium, he also finds that turnover and unrecognized capital gains are negatively related. As a result of high turnover, funds generally have little or no unrecognized gains, and it is the latter factor that appears to be associated with the higher premium/lower discount. The other factors have no ability to explain the cross-sectional variation in the end of 1994 discounts/premiums.

Pontiff, Jeffrey. "Costly Arbitrage: Evidence from Closed-End Fund Discounts." *Quarterly Journal of Economics* 107 (November 1996): 1135-1151.

The author contends that closed-end funds provide a ready vehicle for examining mis-pricing in financial markets. In the spirit of Shiller (1984) and De Long, et al. (1990), the author suggests that the irrational actions of noise traders can lead to prolonged and pronounced deviations from an efficient market equilibrium, in spite of the existence of rational investors. Further, the author contends that rational investors will try to profit from irrational pricing by noise-traders when the benefit of such actions outweighs the costs.

He argues that the ability to exploit closed-end fund discounts is made too costly when the fund's portfolio is difficult to mimic, when interest rates are high, when the bid-ask spread is high, and when the dividend income from the fund's portfolio is low. Using the price of the fund's shares as a proxy for the bid-ask spread (which is seen to rise with share price in other studies), quarterly dividend yield, and the residuals from a prior regression that finds correlation between changes in closed-end fund NAVs and changes in open-end funds NAVs, Pontiff estimates a multi-variate regression model of closed-end fund discounts.

He finds that all of the proposed causal factors enter the estimated relation with the proper sign. While most of the variables have low statistical significance (the residuals/portfolio uniqueness factor being the exception), the overall model explains about a quarter of discount mis-pricing. The author explains that because closed-end country fund portfolios would be difficult to mimic, one should expect their discounts to be larger and more variable than domestic funds.

Finally, Pontiff contends that the premiums observed on municipal bond closed-end funds are largely a result of market frictions. Short-sellers of municipal bond funds could replicate the dividend payment (made to the lender of the shares), but not its tax-exempt status. As a result, Pontiff argues that short selling of closed-end municipal bond funds should be virtually non-existent.

Neal, Robert and Simon Wheatley. "Adverse Selection and Bid-Ask Spreads: Evidence From Closed-End Funds." *Journal of Financial Markets* 1 (1998): 121-149.

A central theme in the financial literature is the notion that insiders and market participants have differential information, thus differential views on value. Models of market clearing in the presence of information asymmetries usually suggest that market makers increase the bid/ask spread they quote for a security when they have less than full information. The increase in the spread protects the broker against arbitrage activities by informed investors.

In the case of closed-end funds (CEICs), the authors argue that the weekly reporting of closed-end funds' net asset value (NAV) should eliminate the difference between the share's price and the liquidation value of the share (NAV). As a result, the adverse-selection component of the bid-ask spread due to information asymmetry should be small for CEICs. This analysis does not argue that the discount should be zero. Rather, the authors argue that the adverse-selection component of the spread should be small, ceteris paribus.

Neal and Wheatley utilize a sample of 17 closed-end funds and a matched set of 17 common stocks from 1988. They require that the funds be publicly traded for more than one calendar year to avoid the increase in discount that often occurs during a fund's seasoning period. The control stocks match the size (i.e., the same rank-ordered decile) and closely approximate the trading volume of their respective funds.

With intra-day trading data, the authors estimate two models of the adverse selection component of the bid-ask spread for the funds and stock counterparts. They report large estimates for the adverse-selection component of the spread for the closed-end funds. However, the size of the component declines during the trading-day, consistent with the notion that information flows help to reduce intra-day asymmetries.

The CEIC evidence seems inconsistent with the notion that frequent publication of the fund's NAV reduces the adverse-selection problem. They examine a number of other hypotheses for the apparently large size of the adverse selection estimate. The authors find no support for an order-flow persistence, takeover activity, portfolio turnover/expense, or insider trading explanation of the size of the component estimate.

The analysis also includes an examination of the relation between the estimate and the size of the fund's discount and its variability. If the investor sentiment hypothesis holds and is systematic, one would expect either the discount or its volatility to be a systematic influence. Their failure to obtain empirical evidence of a systematic influence suggests that the investor sentiment hypothesis is either invalid or unsystematic.

Although the authors find that adverse-selection accounts for about 19% of the bid/ask spread on closed-end funds (about 2.5 cents), the mean estimate for the matched pairs is 34% (about 5.5 cents). The findings for the matched pairs are below those reported in broader studies of non-fund common stocks, and the difference is not trivial. The authors conclude that either the adverse-selection estimation models and evidence are incorrect or that factors other than information asymmetry are responsible for a significant amount of the adverse-selection component estimates that have been previously reported.

Lofthouse, Stephen. "Closed-End Fund and Investment Trust Discounts." *Journal of Investing* (Spring 1999): 27-37.

Investment trusts (ITs) are investment vehicles that trade on U.K. capital markets. Like closed-end funds, most ITs are sold to the public at a small premium to their net asset value (NAV) but soon slump to a discount. On rare occasions "seasoned" ITs trade at a premium to their NAV, but for the most part they trade at discounts like their American closed-end investment company (CEIC) cousins. However, the tax treatment of ITs differs significantly from CEICs.

To maintain their tax-exempt status, ITs must payout at least 85% of the dividend and interest income that they receive. In the U.S., CEICs need to payout 95% of income, regardless of the source. While there are potential tax complications from foreign-source income, ITs can generally avoid any unfavorable withholding taxes with a strong payout policy.

ITs can avoid capital gain taxes only if they are not distributed -- exactly opposite of the U.S. treatment. U.K. shareholders pay capital gains taxes when they liquidate their shares in the IT (which presumably increases in value if the trust has recognized capital gains) at a price above their basis. Thus, Lofthouse argues that the tax-trading hypothesis offered to explain discounts on CEICs would not appear to hold in the U.K. -- where discounts to NAV abound.

Lofthouse also argues that the noise-trader hypothesis of closed-end fund discounts would require that most CEICs shares be held by small investors, who are presumably the most likely noise traders. In the case of ITs, Lofthouse finds that on average only about 20% of their shares are owned by small investors, while the bulk are owned by institutions or management. The author argues that this pattern of ownership does not support a noise-trader hypothesis of discounts for ITs and, thus, undermines the strength of this explanation for CEICs pricing.

Finally, Lofthouse examines the recent history of arbitrage activities in IT shares and finds a number of funds have been taken over or reorganized. Cash takeovers have generally been achieved at 95% to 98% of NAV while other takeovers have involved share swaps. Share buy-backs by ITs are highly regulated, but not impossible. Unitization (i.e., conversion to an open-end fund) has also occurred with some regularity. The variety of avenues available to exploit differences between IT share prices and NAV, combined with the regularity at which takeovers occur, is at odds with the hypothesis that the lack of arbitrage activities explains IT, and by extension, CEIC discounts.

Chay, J.B. and Charles A. Trzcinka. "Managerial performance and the cross-sectional pricing of closed-end funds." *Journal of Financial Economics* 52.2 (1999): 379-408.

The authors test the hypothesis that closed-end fund premiums reflect the expected future investment performance of the fund. They argue that closed-end funds are professionally managed for fees assessed for those services. It follows that shareholders should be willing to pay a relative premium for the shares of funds that are expected to have superior performance net of expenses in future periods. Although Malkiel (1977) found no statistical evidence of a linkage between premiums and future performance, he uses past or current performance as a proxy for expected future performance.

The authors argue that Malkiel's measure of future performance is flawed and propose new methods. In addition, the authors cite an extensive literature that has developed on the "hot hands" of certain investment managers. These studies suggest that investors may develop expectations of future performance and translate those expectations into demand for closed-end funds. Those funds expected to out-perform (under-perform) their peers should be expected to have the smallest (largest) discounts. The authors note that the managerial performance hypothesis is unable to explain cyclical patterns in closed-end fund IPOs.

They compute monthly changes in the net asset values (NAVs) for a sample of 94 stock closed-end funds and 22 closed-end bond funds between 1966 and 1993. With the use of different benchmarks and different risk adjustments, the authors examine a variety of hypotheses relating to investment performance. In general they find a strong positive relation between the level of a fund's premium and the next year's NAV performance for stock funds, but not for bond funds.

Because these results differ so strongly from Lee, et al. (1991), the authors examine a number of other hypotheses that might explain this inconsistency. Chay and Trzcinka include closed-end bond funds in their study; whereas Lee, et al. and others examine only stock funds. Holding out bond funds, Chay and Trzcinka find the relation between premiums and future performance strengthened for equity closed-end funds. The authors note that the relation between gross future NAV performance and premiums has no ability to predict stock fund expenses.

They conclude that strong managerial performance allows the average investor in low discount closed-end funds to recover approximately 78% of the relative premium that they paid if they held the fund for three years. Although unable to explain the total premium for better performing funds, the managerial performance hypothesis is an addition to the understanding of closed-end fund discounts. The authors find that no other aspect of fund pricing or past performance has a statistically significant ability to explain future performance.

Malhotra, D.K. and Robert W. McLeod. "Closed-End Fund Expenses and Investment Selection." *The Financial Review* 41.1 (Spring 2000): 85-104.

Malhotra and McLeod engage in a two-part study of closed-end fund expense ratios. First, the authors produce an empirical model to predict the level of expense ratios in the period 1989 through 1996. Second, the authors look for the relation between fund expense ratios and return performance.

They relate yearly cross-sectional differences in the fund expense ratios (total expenses/total asset value) to: type of fund (stock or bond), domicile of firm issuing the securities (domestic or foreign), size of the fund, age of the fund, and total return of the fund. The authors find that bond funds systematically have lower expense ratios than stock funds, exhibit lower volatility in returns, and are younger. Within stock funds, domestic funds have systematically lower expense ratios than funds that specialize in foreign investments. In addition, domestic funds have a lower volatility in returns and are older than their foreign counterparts.

The authors then examine the expense behavior of stand-alone funds compared with members of a "family" of funds. Fund families exploit economies of scale, but only when the number of funds exceeds five. In general, the authors find that older funds have lower expense ratios, which may be a result of the experience of their managers. However, these savings can be offset if the fund engages in a significant amount of trading turnover.

The relation between changes in the fund's NAV and expense ratio is relatively weak, although statistically significant in five of the seven years examined. The slope coefficient on the performance variable is significant in five of the seven periods, but the coefficient is positive and significant in only two of the five periods. In the other periods there is either no relation or they find that lower expenses are associated with higher returns. As with a myriad of other studies, this work fails to convincingly support the hypothesis that professional investment management yields benefits greater than its cost.

Coles, Jeffery, Jose Suay and Denise Woodbury. "Fund Advisor Compensation in Closed-End Funds." *Journal of Finance* 55.3 (June 2000): 1385-1414

This paper analyzes compensation schemes employed by closed-end funds. The authors seek to determine how these contracts may influence the structure, pricing, NAV performance, and share price performance of closed-end funds. They also address the relation between closed-end fund discounts and the compensation scheme employed by the fund.

Coles, et al. analyze the available annual performance of 81 externally managed closed-end funds over the period 1978 to 1991. A total of 71 fund advisors are associated with these funds during the sample period. The total data sample of 425 year-end observations comprises 326 bond fund and 99 stock fund observations.

The authors report that 55% of the fund managers are compensated with a "flat" rate based on the value of net assets under management. The remaining advisors in the sample are compensated by a declining marginal rate based on the value of net assets under management. They report that only a small percentage of funds employ schemes that benchmark the performance of the advisors. However, they do report that a large number of contracts contain clauses that make adjustments to compensation when either expenses or income are excessive.

In their examination of the relation between a closed-end fund's discount and elements of the compensation scheme, they also make adjustments for the ownership position of the advisors. In general, the authors report that discounts on closed-end funds decline as the marginal compensation rises. The authors find little evidence that penalties for excess expenses or adjustments for excess income have an influence on the closed-end fund's discount. They do find a positive relation between closed-end fund discounts and the ownership position of the advisory group/directors for stock funds, but not for bond funds.

Rowe, Wei Wang and Wallace N. Davidson III. "Fund Manager Succession in Closed-End Mutual Funds." *Financial Review* 35.3 (August, 2000): 53-78.

Over the past four decades a large volume of research has been devoted to the question of managerial succession, subsequent firm performance, and returns to shareholders. Findings have been contradictory and ambiguous. In this paper, the authors restrict themselves to changes in management in the closed-end fund industry. The authors collect a sample of 102 public announcements of actual changes in management, or announcements that ultimately led to changes in management (e.g., impending retirement), between 1993 and 1995. Changes in management not accompanied by a public announcement are excluded from analysis. The sample is divided between domestic equity funds (23), international equity funds (45), and bond funds (34, 21 of which were municipal bond funds).

Abnormal returns are defined as the actual return less risk-adjusted expected returns. Systematic risk estimators are obtained in the 180 trading-day period that begins 200 days prior to the announcement. With the exception of the 13 taxable bond funds, none of the pre-announcement or announcement period abnormal returns are significantly different from zero.

In the case of taxable bond funds, the replacement of management was associated with a negative return to shareholders.

Decomposition of the announcement effects provides little insight into observed cross-sectional differences. In general, funds with larger discounts respond more positively to news of management change. Conversely, insider ownership has a negative influence on the announcement effect – opposite of what one would predict based on the alignment of shareholder and insider interests.

There is a small difference in announcement effects due to the composition of the board of the directors. However, the authors' find that the composition varies widely by fund type and thus, it is empirically impossible to distinguish between the influence of board composition and fund type. Overall, there are small improvements in performance: expense ratios decline, while portfolio returns increase. However, the average discount increases in the year following the change in management. The mixed nature of the findings and the lack of a significant announcement effect lead the authors to conclude that a change in top management is a "non-event."

Chapter 7

IDIOSYNCRATIC CLOSED-END FUND STUDIES

1. INTRODUCTION

This chapter provides an opportunity to summarize articles that do not fit well into the above three areas of recent closed-end fund research. Several of these papers are idiosyncratic, and others address similar issues such as the returns that can be earned by trading strategies based on the discounts of closed-end fund shares. Yet others address matters ranging from fund IPOs to pedagogy. Here, we also summarize those earlier papers we overlooked in our prior work.

Close, James A. "Investment Companies: Closed-End versus Open-End." *Harvard Business Review* 29 (1952): 79-88.

Close authored the first CEF academic article of which we are aware. In this descriptive work, he discusses the differences between closed-end and open-end funds, and he anticipates many later contributions to the fund literature. Reviewing data on assets under management from 1940-1950, the author reports that the open-end portion of the industry passes in number the closed-end funds by the end of 1943. Further, open-end funds (all 98 of them) have three times the assets of closed-end funds under management by the end of 1950. Close reviews the differences between open and closed-end funds in an effort to determine if there are any structural reasons for the tremendous growth of open-end funds and the relative stagnancy of closed-end funds.

He argues that the great growth in open-end funds is primarily related to the continuous, and well-compensated, sales effort via loads that are undertaken by these funds. In addition, high fixed commission rates on small trades tend to discourage small investments in publicly traded shares, including closed-end funds. Close also contends that the long-standing practice of paying out capital gains by open-end funds could confuse unsophisticated investors.

He notes three aspects of CEFs that should facilitate CEF growth, but that do not. First, CEFs offer investors the ability to buy shares at a substantial discount from NAV, providing a boost to the investor's return if the discount narrows. Second, closed-end funds can make use of leverage, potentially enhancing returns to the common stockholders. Third, closed-end funds do not have to manage inflows/outflows of new funds -- which usually arrive at the wrong time (new money pours in when NAVs are high and flows out when NAVs are low).

Close then analyzes the actual investment performance of a sample of open-end funds (37 of the 98 in existence) and all 11 closed-end funds listed on the NYSE. During the period January 1, 1937, to December 31, 1946, and several sub-periods, the mean NAV returns earned by closed-end fund managers exceed those earned by the sample of open-end fund managers. Close ends with a caution to potential investors to carefully investigate the expense and management fee arrangements for any fund, open- or closed-end, before committing capital.

Marcus, Matityahu and Uzi Yaari. "How a Closed-End Fund Can Out-Perform Its Own Stock Portfolio." *International Journal of Finance* 1.1 (Autumn, 1988): 1-14.

The Investment Company Act of 1940 allows funds to be exempt from federal income tax as long as they pass through 95% of their dividend/interest income and their net capital gains. The authors show that under certain circumstances a fund could earn a higher after-tax return on a portfolio of securities than its shareholders could earn by directly investing in the securities, even when the fund elects to retain income and pay federal income taxes on that income. In the absence of special circumstances, the shareholders of the fund would be subject to an additional layer of taxes.

The authors argue that the source of the gain results from the opportunity of the investment company to reinvest the income received from its underlying portfolio at a rate of return that might exceed the return required by its investors. If the investment company can capture the value added from such an investment policy, the net gain above the tax penalty to its shareholders could be positive. Once the possibility of such an arbitrage is possible, the value of the investment company becomes an increasing function of the percentage of its income that it retains. The ability to arbitrage suggests that the fund should minimize its portfolio turnover, thus minimizing its brokerage charges and maximizing the amount of funds that it can invest in the arbitrage activity.

The authors provide a variety of numerical examples based on the tax code before and after the major changes in 1986. While there is no question that the model prepared by the authors is correct, they do not explore the kinds of conditions that must hold for the arbitrage to exist. For example, a necessary condition would appear to require at least a lag (of one period or more) in the ability of investors to observe the underlying risk of the fund's portfolio. If the fund's portfolio were transparent, it would appear impossible for the discount rate applied to the fund's shares to systematically deviate from the average discount rate of the fund's portfolio.

Peavy, John W. III. "Closed-End Fund IPOs: Caveat Emptor."
Financial Analysts Journal (May/June, 1989): 71-75.

This is another article omitted from our first volume. Although we were aware of the existence of this piece as a working paper when we started our first volume, we were unaware that the paper had appeared in print prior to our work's completion.

In this perhaps the earliest study of closed-end fund IPOs, the author documents their unusual behavior. Peavy reports that the 34 new closed-end funds in his sample sell at an average 7.54% premium to net asset value. The author also reports that the first-day return on these funds is a miniscule 0.88%, which is not significantly different from zero. This is in sharp contrast to the strong first-day returns reported for industrial IPOs.

Upon further examination, Peavy finds that 3 of the 34 funds received special permission to invest in foreign markets that were off-limits to U.S.-based investors. Not surprisingly, these three funds experience a first-day return of +21.11%. The remaining 31 funds in his sample have a mean first-day return of -1.08%.

He reports that the cumulative raw and market-adjusted returns to investors in the first 100 trading days (excluding day 1) are negative. Much of the poor performance can be attributed to the behavior of the fund's premium -- not the actual investment performance of the fund. After opening with an average premium of 7.54%, the funds close the first 100 days with an average discount of 16.02% -- a decline of 23%. Peavy speculates that the poor performance of these investments is due to the over-sold nature of many of the closed-end fund IPOs.

Schnabel, Jacques A. "Corporate Spin-Offs and Closed-End Funds in a State-Preference Framework." *Financial Review* 27.3 (August 1992): 391-409.

Using an Arrow-Debreu state-preference model, the author provides rigorous support for the positions held in a series of articles by Edward Miller (1977, 1978, and 1989). In those articles Miller argues that if short-selling is restricted, the price of risky assets will be driven above the prices they would reach in the presence of short-selling. Further, Miller argues that the sum of the values that the individual parts of a firm (or individual assets for a closed-end fund) would likely exceed the value that investors would pay for the whole of the firm or the portfolio of the closed-end fund. These assertions made by Miller appear to explain why closed-end fund shares sell at discounts from their net asset value (NAV) for prolonged periods of time and why other firms experience increases in share price when divestitures are announced. The discounts and/or gains from spin-off announcements appear to be in excess of what could be explained by "rational" hypotheses (transactions costs and wealth expropriation of bondholders, respectively, as examples).

Schnabel demonstrates that value additivity will not hold in a world where a short-selling constraint is binding. Moreover, he demonstrates that if a short-selling constraint is not binding, value additivity will result regardless of whether expectations are heterogeneous or whether utility functions are state-dependent. Put differently, investor clienteles may develop in such a market, but they will not systematically impact asset pricing (i.e., discounts will not result, nor will gains be achieved by announcing divestitures). Finally, Schnabel suggests that tax-timing options will exist, regardless of a binding short-sale restriction.

Caks, John and Emilio R. Zarruk. "Closed-End Fund Discounts: Pedagogical Note." *Financial Practice and Education* (Spring/Summer 1993): 95-97.

In this brief paper, the authors argue that management fees and other costs act as a drain on the possible cash disbursements from dividend income by a closed-end fund. If the fund is not expected to liquidate in a reasonable period of time, the shares of the fund would be expected to sell at a discount to their net asset value (NAV) per share. The amount of discount would be equal to the amount of the costs, discounted by the expected return for the fund, which should be a weighted average of expected returns for the underlying assets.

The authors construct a small sample of seven closed-end funds and compute the average expense ratio for the funds from 1976-1986, which is 0.75%. Discounted by the average dividend yield of the S & P 500, the authors generate a set of "justifiable" discounts that range between 13% and 21% during the period, with an average of 17%. The discounts for the seven funds in the sample range from 6% to 26%, with an average of 14%. The authors make additional adjustments for capital gain distributions to obtain a final range of discount estimates.

Pontiff, Jeffrey. "Closed-end Fund Premia and Returns: Implications for Financial Market Equilibrium." *Journal of Financial Economics* 37 (1995): 341-370.

The author re-examines the empirical relation between the discounts on closed-end funds and their subsequent returns. He clearly delineates that the paper is not an attempt to explain either the level or changes in discounts. Rather, the author is troubled by the apparent pay-off of trading rules developed for closed-end funds based on their discount from their net asset value (NAV). After documenting the predicting power of closed-end fund discounts, Pontiff searches for an explanation for their predictive power.

The author finds strong evidence that shareholders of funds with large (small) discounts earn large (small) returns on their investment. Discounts are not found to predict subsequent changes in the fund NAV. Consistent with other authors, Pontiff reports that the source of the return to stockholders is primarily the mean-reverting nature of the discount.

Pontiff attempts to explain the ability of the discounts to predict future movements in the prices of closed-end fund shares. He relates movements in the excess returns to the month of the year (i.e., the January effect), dividend yield on the fund's portfolio, a measure of the bid-ask spread, the systematic risk of the fund's portfolio, and level of discounts. The author finds that discounts are a significant explanatory variable. Pontiff finds that the January effect explains more of the variance in closed-end fund returns than the book-to-market value ratio impact documented by Fama and French (*Journal of Financial Economics*, 1993).

Peavy, John W. III. "New Evidence on the Turn-of-the-Year Effect from Closed-End Fund IPOs." *Journal of Financial Services Research* 9.1 (1995): 49-64.

The author states that one of the most persistent anomalies in financial markets is the so-called "January" effect. Prior research documents an abnormal positive return to stockholders in the month of January, as compared with the other eleven months of the year. This impact appears to be stronger for firms with small market values. Peavy proposes to examine the returns to the shareholders of recently floated closed-end funds (CEFs) in an effort to determine what may be at the heart of the January effect.

With a sample of 71 closed-end funds that went public between 1986 and 1990, Peavy examines the behavior of returns in their first year of public trading and in their first January. As reported in other venues, the initial returns to shareholders of new closed-end funds are negative. Institutional ownership in the new CEFs is limited. However, average returns to shareholders in the first few days of January are positive.

Peavy places the funds into size-ranked portfolios and finds that the smallest CEFs experience the most negative shareholder returns in their first year of public trading. He also finds that the smallest CEFs experience the largest early-January rally. This result seems to be driven more by tax-loss selling the prior December than as a result of the size of the fund. In a cross-sectional regression, fund size is insignificant, but prior year returns are highly significant in explaining early January returns. This evidence strongly supports the tax-loss selling hypothesis, but not the firm-size hypothesis.

Weiss Hanley, Kathleen, Charles M.C. Lee, and Paul J. Seguin. "The Marketing of Closed-End Fund IPOs: Evidence from Transactions Data." *Journal of Financial Intermediation* 5.1 (Spring 1996): 127-159.

The authors note that closed-end funds experience a -12.6% excess return in the five months following their IPO; whereas industrial and manufacturing firms experience an 18.5% excess return in the same period following their IPO. If the market were rational, investors would incorporate this information into their demand for closed-end fund IPOs. In such a market, new funds would not be brought to market, let alone at a premium to the net asset value (NAV). Also, most of this decline begins to occur after 30 trading days following the IPO. This begs the question of why the shares do not immediately decline in value in light of the large underwriting expenses categorizing closed-end fund IPOs.

The authors examine after-market transactions for fund IPOs and document sell-to-buy imbalances by large traders, transactions in excess of $10,000 market value. The high underwriting fees earned by members of the syndicate encourage them to sell to large sophisticated investors who have no long-term interest in owning the shares but who hope to earn a short-term profit by "flipping." The lead underwriter faces a difficult time trying to police members of the syndicate stabilizing the price of the new offering, without losing reputation capital or their share of the underwriting fees.

Weiss, et al. document a sharp decline in the prices of closed-end fund IPOs once the underwriting support period has ended. In addition, the authors demonstrate that funds have negative cumulative excess returns at day +100 following the IPO date. Nearly three-fourths of the decline is experienced on a single day, which almost always occurs after the underwriting stabilization period ends. The authors also find that the bid-ask spread increases following the stabilization period.

They report that those funds with the strongest selling pressure in the first few days of trading experience the greatest declines in the first few weeks. They also demonstrate a strong relation between the duration of stabilization activities and the exercise of over-allotment options. While this may seem curious, it is not. When flipping is unexpectedly low, the syndicate members find it profitable to exercise over-allotment options in order to satisfy the strong demand. This keeps members of the syndicate "active" in the underwriting process longer than they would be in the absence of the demand that led to the exercising of the over-allotment options. Not surprisingly, shares of funds that have no options exercised experience their first drop in share price at day +24; whereas funds with exercised options experience their first price drop at day +35. This difference grows with the rate at which options are exercised.

The authors contend that virtually everything about the closed-end fund IPO process smacks of sophisticated professionals taking advantage of unsophisticated investors. Closed-end country fund IPOs appear marginally less damaging to small investors than their "domestic" counterparts.

The authors conclude that closed-end fund IPO behavior is best explained by a "profitability to underwriters who market" hypothesis. The authors find that flippers and small investors participate in the IPO, but it is the small investors who are left holding the bag when the music stops (i.e., the price stabilization activities are abandoned).

Arak, Marcelle and Dean Taylor. "Risk and Return in Trading Closed-End Country Funds: Can Trading Beat Holding Foreign Stocks?"
The Quarterly Review of Economics and Finance 36.2 (1996): 219-231.

The authors examine two aspects of closed-end country funds' (CECFs) discounts. First, the authors examine the mean-reversion behavior of discounts. Do large discounts "naturally and predictably" decline to some level (e.g., zero)? Second, the authors examine the ability of discount-based trading rules to produce returns that exceed those earned either by a buy-and-hold strategy for the fund's shares or by its portfolio.

Arak and Taylor extend the previous works of Richards, Fraser and Groth (RFG) (1980) and Anderson (1987). The authors construct a "filter rule" that provides them a model for timing the decision to actively alter one's portfolio. They sell a previously owned portfolio of foreign stock that is identical to the CECF when the discount on the fund reaches a given level. The proceeds are used to take a position in the CECF's shares. Those shares will be held until the discount declines to a given level.

The authors compute the long-term average discount for a sample of 15 funds from 1986 to 1991. They omit CECFs if the market is closed to foreign investors (e.g., Korea and Brazil) because it would be impossible for investors to purchase the fund's underlying portfolio. They report a grand-mean average discount of 9.4%, with a standard deviation of 10.4% and also report evidence that discounts on these funds exhibit strong autocorrelation--the discounts are mean reverting.

Investors are assumed to purchase the fund's portfolio when the fund's discount reaches 9.4% and sell those shares when the discount increases to 19.8% (mean less one standard deviation). The proceeds from the sale of these securities are invested in the CECF's shares, holding them until the discount declines to the mean (9.4%). Because of the behavior of the discounts during the sample period, the trading rule yields buy-and-sell decisions that are qualitatively closed to the rule of "buying when the discount is 20% and selling with the discount narrows to 10%" that was examined by both RFG and Anderson.

The authors assume a 4% commission charge to achieve the active strategy defined by the trading rule. They report that the strategy outperforms a simple buy-and-hold strategy for the funds' portfolios by 23%. Because CECF returns and premiums are positively correlated with U.S. market returns, the authors examine the systematic risk of CECFs to determine if the class of funds is extraordinarily risky. The authors compute the fund's share price and NAV betas with a single index model and find the average share price beta to be slightly greater than one. Making a risk-adjustment to their excess return measure, the authors argue that their trading strategy outperforms a simple buy-and-hold by 21.8%.

Arak, Marcell and Dean Taylor. "Optimal trading with mean-reverting prices: switching between foreign stocks and closed-end country funds." *Applied Economics* 28 (1996): 1067-1074.

The authors begin with a restatement of the law of one price arguing that investors will engage in arbitrage when the difference in the asset's price in two markets differs by more than the transactions costs necessary to undertake the arbitrage transaction. They contend that closed-end funds appear to violate the arbitrage profit rule. The authors observe that shares of closed-end funds trade at pronounced discounts from their net asset value (NAV) for prolonged periods of time, and the discounts are much larger than can be explained by arbitrage transactions costs alone.

They extend the noise trader hypothesis to suggest that rational trading rules based on closed-end fund discounts may produce substantial profits. The authors suggest that trading one security (e.g., the closed-end fund's shares) for another (e.g., the closed-end fund's portfolio) is akin to exercising an option -- including the loss of the remaining time value of the option. However, the act of buying the second asset (e.g., the portfolio) gains the investor a new option to "switch back."

Modeling the switch decision as an American option, they examine the conditions under which the exercise should occur. The key parameters are the volatility of the underlying assets, the expected rate of convergence between the two assets' prices, and the level of transactions costs. Not surprisingly, the authors find that the greater the volatility and transactions costs, the larger the price disparity (i.e., discount) must be to justify a switch. Also, the slower the convergence rate, the greater the price disparity must be in order to justify the switch.

They present evidence on the mean-reverting nature of closed-end fund discounts. Making use of these estimates and various one-way transactions cost estimates, the authors estimate the minimum closed-end fund discount that is needed to justify the purchase of the fund's shares (assuming the sale of the underlying portfolio). For example, if commissions are 2% and weekly volatility in the fund's portfolio is 5%, the optimal buy point for a closed-end fund is an 8.4% discount from equilibrium (when the discount has a mean-reversion of 15% per week), and the optimal sell is at an 8.4%

premium to the equilibrium. Each fund's equilibrium discount rate can be unique (e.g., the mean level could serve as an estimate of the equilibrium rate).

Arak and Taylor examine the ability of their estimated trading strategy to generate excess returns for a sample of 15 funds. They report long average holding periods of approximately four years between switches for the closed-end fund's common stock for the trading rule. The rules generate excess returns in 12 of the 15 cases where a trade occurred. The average excess return is 5%-7% annually.

Chance, Don M. "A Theory of the Value of Active Investment Management and Its Implications for Closed-End Funds and Investment Management Contracts." *Advances in Financial Economics* 3.2 (1997): 81-115.

This paper addresses the question of whether there is a difference between the ex-ante value of a passive portfolio and the ex-ante value of an actively managed portfolio. Does the expectation of trading securities add or destroy value? The author clearly demonstrates that in an efficient market, the expectation of trading destroys value, above and beyond the transactions costs of the trading.

Chance models the behavior of an active portfolio manager who attempts to identify under-priced portfolios from a set of portfolios known to be mis-priced. Investors are assumed to have a logarithmic utility function. This function implies many investor behaviors that are desirable because they are closely aligned with those we observe in the market. These behaviors include: non-satiable, risk aversion, decreasing absolute risk aversion, and constant relative risk aversion. These are partially offset by the undesirable property that one unit of wealth provides the same utility to all investors, irrespective of their wealth.

The concave nature of log utility functions yields critical insights into the market pricing of closed-end funds (CEICs). In an efficient market where the chance of identifying an undervalued portfolio is 50/50, the likelihood of identifying an overvalued portfolio by mistake is also 50/50. If the return on the undervalued portfolio is equal to –1 times the return on the overvalued portfolio, the expected return of active management is zero. However, utility gained from the active management is less than the utility of making no trades – even if the trades are costless. Because of the lower utility, investors would be willing to hold shares of actively managed CEICs only if they sell at a discount.

In order to generate a prediction of fund shares selling at a premium to NAV, one must make one or more "aggressive" assumptions. One might assume that gains from an undervalued portfolio are greater than losses incurred from an overvalued portfolio (a non-symmetric distribution of returns). Alternately, the probability of correctly identifying an undervalued portfolio is greater than 50%. However, with a variety of numerical examples, the author demonstrates that a 57% success rate with symmetric returns is necessary to produce a discount of zero, even when transactions costs are equal to zero.

In summary, the author demonstrates that the discounts that characterize closed-end funds are a logical result from active portfolio management in a costly market that can be characterized as efficient. He contends that it takes either irrationality or the expectation of a dramatically good investment selection to justify paying a premium for closed-end fund shares. Ironically, the model developed here makes it more difficult to explain the existence of open-end funds, which must be purchased at NAV, than it does closed-end funds.

Sias, Richard William. "Optimum Trading Strategies for Closed-End Funds." *Journal of Investing* (Spring 1997): 54-61.

The author notes that a number of academic and professional investors have written on trading rule strategy returns using closed-end funds. The size of these returns exceeds anything that can be explained by transactions costs or extra risk. These results appear to be a result of mean-reversion in closed-end fund discounts. In addition, the author notes that the results appear to be sensitive to the weighting scheme used to determine the positions that are taken in the closed-end fund shares and/or portfolio when a "switch" signal is obtained from the trading rule.

The author collects monthly returns to shareholders of 57 closed-end funds, changes in the fund's underlying portfolio, and the difference between the fund's price and net asset value (NAV) from July 1965 to December 1989. He argues that returns to shareholders of closed-end funds can be decomposed into the return on the fund's portfolio and the return on changes in the fund's discount. The latter component represents the return that can be earned as result of the mean-reverting behavior of closed-end fund discounts.

Sias examines a simple trading rule: buy funds that are selling at a price below their NAV. The author applies different weights to the securities that the investor hypothetically purchases. The following trading rule schemes are proposed: (1) an equal weight for each fund selling at a discount, (2) a discount-weighting scheme (w = discount/sum of the discounts) that puts more wealth into funds with the largest discount, and (3) a different power weight for each weight in (2).

The author demonstrates that the returns to the simple discount weighting are 4% higher than a simple equally-weight scheme. In addition, the author shows that abnormal returns grow as the exponent applied to the discount-weight grows. Sias demonstrates that the change in excess returns declines monotonically as the exponents grow. Put differently, investors can earn increasing amounts of excess return as they invest greater amounts of their wealth in funds with the largest discounts.

Klibanoff, Peter, Owen Lamont, and Thierry A. Wizman. "Investor Reaction to Salient News in Closed-End Country Funds." *Journal of Finance* 52.2 (April 1998): 673-699.

The authors examine the reaction of closed-end country fund (CF) share prices to changes in their portfolio's net asset value (NAV) from 1984 to 1994. Reporting conventions in the U.S. require reporting the NAV value for closed-end funds only at the close of trading on Friday; whereas open-end funds are reported daily. Of interest is whether intra-week returns anticipate actual changes in NAV based on observable movements in local market indices during the week. Initial results suggest that a contemporaneous movement in the CF's share price captures only 64% of the movement in NAV.

The authors examine the hypothesis that the reporting of CF country-related news items on the front page of the *New York Times* (*NYT*) should not change the reaction functions. Put differently, the *NYT* reporting should be redundant if NAV responses are efficient. The evidence does not support the redundancy hypothesis, as the share price response relative to changes in the NAV is stronger/more complete in weeks where news items appear on page one in the *NYT* than in other weeks.

The authors examine differences in trading volume (news vs. non-news weeks) and find a substantial increase in weeks where news items are reported on the front page of the *NYT*. This evidence is consistent with the hypothesized behavior of noise-traders. They test a number of alternative hypotheses (e.g., liquid vs. illiquid foreign market influence on NAV changes) to explain the difference in behavior and find no support for other alternatives.

Olienyk, John P., Robert G. Schweback, and J. Kenton Zumwalt. "WEBS, SPDRs, and Country Funds: An Analysis of International Co-integration." *Journal of Multinational Financial Management* 9 (1999): 217-232.

A number of authors have investigated the extent to which national stock indices exhibit positive correlation in their returns. Strong correlation suggests the two markets are "co-integrated," a necessary condition for an equality in the price of market risk across boundaries. An equality in the price of risk across boundaries removes arbitrage profit opportunities and contributes to overall efficiency of the macro economy by ensuring that capital is employed appropriately. However, co-integration virtually eliminates the ability of investors to reduce the risk of their portfolios by making investments in economies whose assets' returns are not perfectly correlated with returns in the domestic economy.

A sub-set of tests for the co-integration in international capital markets have involved closed-end country funds serving as proxies for investments in the market portfolio of the foreign country. The correlation in movement in the closed-end net asset values (NAV) and/or share prices and broad market indices, provides the basis for co-integration tests. However, the use of proxies makes rejection of the co-integration hypothesis problematic because one cannot be certain if the failure to find positive correlation is a result of the use of proxies or the lack of co-integration.

Olienyk, Schwebach, and Zumwalt address this latter difficulty by making use of two new types of securities: WEBS (World Equity Benchmark Shares) and SPDR (Standard and Poor's Depository Receipts). Both securities are similar to closed-end funds, but they serve as "index" funds; whereas closed-end funds can engage in active trading. The authors examine daily returns from March 18, 1996, through October 31, 1998, (n=665) for 17 WEBS, the SPDR, and 12 closed-end country funds.

They employ time-series analysis and conclude that while none of the WEBS and SPDR series is stationary in its level, they are all stationary in first differences (i.e., returns follow a random walk). The authors then conduct a series of pair-wise tests for co-integration and report that 24 out of 45 possible European pairs, 8 out of 10 Asian, and 2 out of 3 North American series exhibit significant co-integration (i.e., contemporaneous correlations are different from zero). The authors note that the U.S. market "Granger-caused" only the Mexican market (WEBS) to move contemporaneously, but that movements in the U.S. market were next-day Granger-caused to move by 13 of the 17 European markets (WEBS) examined.

The authors employ time-series analysis and conclude that the 12 closed-end country fund series are not stationary in levels, but follow a random walk. The authors report substantial support for co-integration between the country-fund returns series and its WEBS series, as one would expect. Interestingly, the authors find evidence of Granger-causal relations between a number of pairs of the closed-end funds. This implies the possibility of constructing trading rules that capture arbitrage profits from these predictable drifts.

Porter, Gary, Rodney L. Roenfeldt, and Neil W. Sicherman. "The Value of Open Market Repurchases of Closed-End Fund Shares." *Journal of Business* 72.2 (1999): 257-276.

Individual closed-end fund managers, industry analysts, and academics, offer a number of motivations for the open-market repurchase of closed-end fund (CEIC) shares. If the purchase takes place while the shares are selling at a discount to net asset value (NAV), the act will enhance the NAV of the remaining shares through the capture of the discount. In addition, some argue that the repurchase signals the true value of the fund's shares. Finally, one can argue that a repurchase program may sufficiently shift the demand for the shares so as to reduce or eliminate the discount.

Porter, Roenfeldt, and Sicherman employ a sample of 27 open-market repurchase announcements by closed-end funds in the period 1986 through 1995. The percentage of outstanding shares to be repurchased ranges from 3.2% to 26.7%, with a mean of 9.4%. The repurchase plans are slightly larger than are typically reported for industrial firms.

The authors develop a model that predicts the amount of re-pricing that should accompany an offer to repurchase shares. This amount is roughly equal to the amount of the discount times the percentage of shares to be retired. Regressing two-day actual returns at the time of the announcement against this expected return, the authors obtain a slope coefficient that is different from zero and not different from one. This evidence is consistent with the hypothesis that the market prices out the capture of the discount, but there is no evidence of an additional signaling effect.

They expand the analysis of the announcement effect and find that the fund size and pre-announcement trading volume fail to improve the explanatory power of the model. In addition, the authors find no evidence that the repurchase reduces the discount below what would be predicted by the repurchase of the shares and capture of the discount. Finally, unlike industrial firms, the authors find a positive relation between the amount of pre-announcement excess returns and the subsequent re-pricing of the closed-end funds.

Bers, Martina K. and Jeff Madura. "The Performance Persistence of Closed-End Funds." *Financial Review* 35.3 (August, 2000): 33-52.

The authors extend the literature on performance persistence in the mutual fund industry to closed-end funds. The authors compile a sample of 384 domestic closed-end funds for the period January 1976 (or inception) to December 1996. The majority of these funds are bond funds, municipal (n =

202), and taxable (n = 115); while the minority are equity (n = 67) funds. Returns to stockholders, returns on the fund's portfolio, and the discount/premium of the funds are measured monthly.

They measure abnormal performance with Jensen's (1968) alpha. The benchmark employed (e.g., S&P 500 for equity funds) differs by the type of fund being analyzed. To compute the persistence in performance, the abnormal return metric (alpha) in a subsequent period is regressed against the metric in the current period. A slope coefficient different from zero in this latter regression would be evidence consistent with the hypothesis that performance persists.

Over the entire period examined, equity funds had higher monthly returns to stockholders and on their portfolio than taxable bond funds or municipal bond funds. While the average rates of return to stockholders and to NAV were virtually identical for equity and taxable bond funds, the average monthly return to stockholders of municipal bond funds was 15 basis points below the NAV return (0.49% vs. 0.64%). Using 24 and 36-month measurement periods, the authors find some evidence of positive abnormal performance for the NAVs of equity funds. Neither the taxable nor municipal bond fund sub-samples yield evidence of abnormal performance.

Estimation of performance persistence was more revealing. In the case of taxable bond funds the authors find strong evidence of positive performance persistence in the fund's portfolio looking 12, 24, and 36 months into the future. However, the authors detect statistically significant persistence in share price performance only for the 36-month window.

In the case of municipal bond funds, the evidence is mixed. The authors report significant negative persistence in the 12-month period, but positive persistence in the 24-month figure (consistent with mean-reversion) when measured on the NAV. Price performance persistence is positive and significant for the 12-month period.

The strongest evidence is obtained for the equity funds. The authors report extremely strong persistence in NAV performance in the 12, 24, and 36-month periods. This persistence is matched in strength and sign by share price persistence. The authors conclude that investment managers for equity and taxable bond funds exhibit strong positive performance persistence in their portfolios, but only the stockholders of equity funds are rewarded with strong positive performance on the funds' shares.

Chapter 8

SUMMARY OF FINDINGS

In this chapter, we briefly summarize each paper reviewed and group them into specific areas. This grouping is somewhat arbitrary because many papers are multi-faceted. Our purpose is to provide the reader with a concise, perhaps too concise, summary of findings for each primary sub-area of research over the past decade.

1. INVESTOR SENTIMENT

1.1 Supporting evidence

Lee, et al. (Fall 1990) argue that the behavior of noise traders may provide an explanation for the level and variability of discounts and for the cyclical pattern of closed-end fund IPOs.

Lee, et al. (March 1991) find a positive relation between small firm returns and the narrowing of closed-end fund discounts and contend that this finding supports the sentiment hypothesis.

De Long, et al. (September 1991) argue that the large premiums on closed-end funds during the late 1920s support the noise trader hypothesis.

De Long, et al. (Winter 1992) review closed-end fund discount behavior during the 1980s and conclude that discounts are an index of small investor sentiment.

Chopra, et al. (June 1993) again report that changes in fund discount explain much of the variation in small firm share returns.

Bodurtha, et al. (1995) investigate the association between country fund discounts, U.S. stock returns, total market returns, and other variables. They find that small firms and funds may be substitutes and conclude that noise traders impact discounts.

Noronha and Rubin (Summer, 1995) employ a multifactor model to investigate discount factors, which yields conflicting results. They conclude that discounts' changes are a function of investor sentiment.

Sias (1997) investigates the association between fund discount and several economic and sentiment variables. He finds that six economic variables explain only 12% of fund discount variability and concludes that his findings support Lee, et al.

Klibanoff, et al. (April 1998) find that country fund shares capture only 64% of the movement in NAV and conclude that this supports the investor sentiment hypothesis.

Neal and Wheatley (December 1998) find a positive relationship between fund discount changes and future small firm returns. These findings are consistent with the investor sentiment hypothesis.

Brown (March/April 1999) finds that changes in an investor sentiment variable are associated with increases in fund variability and concludes that this finding supports the investor sentiment hypothesis.

1.2 Conflicting evidence

Brauer (1993) determines that the proportion of changes in discounts in closed-end funds attributable to noise traders amounts to approximately 7%.

Chen, et al. (June 1993) investigate the association between small firm returns and changes in fund discounts and conclude that their evidence refutes the investor sentiment hypothesis.

Swaminathan (1996) finds that fund discounts have some ability to predict real earnings and concludes that his finding does not support the irrationality inherent in the noise-trader hypothesis.

Sias (Summer 1997) investigates order-flow imbalance and determines that noise-traders do not create risk for institutional traders. He concludes that his findings do not support the irrational behavior hypothesis ascribed to small investors.

Abraham, et al. (1998) investigate both bond and stock fund discounts and find a measure of discount volatility to be the same for both. They conclude that this finding does not support the investor sentiment hypothesis.

Kramer and Smith (1998) report that Mexico country funds sell at premiums after the 1994 peso-crisis and conclude that this is inconsistent with the investor sentiment hypothesis.

2. CLOSED-END COUNTRY FUNDS

2.1 Investment restriction findings

Bosner-Neal, et al. (June 1990) find that four of the five funds examined exhibit a decrease in price-to-NAV ratios when investment restrictions are relaxed.

Chowdhury (1994) finds that the impact of investment restriction changes on discounts is related to the extent of restriction at the time of the change in policy.

Choi and Lee (1996) find evidence via country funds that markets are segmented when significant barriers to foreign investors exist.

2.2 Market influence evidence

Medewitz, et al. (Spring 1994) report that changes in country fund share price and NAV changes are driven by changes in the market level when the market is well established.

La Barge and La Barge (1996) investigate seven Latin America country funds' returns on a series of mean-variance efficient portfolios and conclude that historic based allocation strategies are highly problematic.

Arshanapalli, et al. (Fall 1996) report that country fund returns are strongly impacted by both their target market and the U.S. market.

Anderson, et al. (Fall 2001) conclude that country fund returns are not so strongly impacted by U.S. market returns as prior studies report.

2.3 Diversification findings

Bailey and Lim (Spring 1992) conclude that funds are a relatively poor vehicle for international diversification.

Johnson, et al. (November/December 1993) find that country funds shares provide less international diversification benefit than does either fund NAV or the target market index.

Chang, et al. (1995) report that efficient frontiers utilizing country fund NAVs dominate frontiers employing country fund shares.

Beckaert and Urias (July 1996) report that U.S. investors' efficient frontiers are more significantly impacted by emerging market country funds traded in the U.K. than by similar funds traded in the U.S.

Errunza, et al. (1998) conclude that country funds are imperfect vehicles for international diversification relative to local indexes.

Ghose and Born (Fall 1998) conclude that country funds appear to be less effective for international diversification that the indexes for the target country market.

3. RATIONAL FACTORS FOR DISCOUNTS

3.1 Taxes

Brickley, et al. (1991) find a positive relation between discounts and the variability of returns as predicted by the extended tax-timing model of Constantinidies.

Kim (Spring 1994) presents a loss of tax-timing model which he argues directly impacts funds' discounts.

Leonard and Shull (Spring 1996) conclude that tax motivations are important for the individual investors who are the primary fund holders.

3.2 Management Fees

Kumar, Raman and Noronha (Summer 1992) find that differences in management fees explain only a small proportion of the cross-sectional variance in fund discounts.

Malhotra and McLeod. (Spring 2000) find weak evidence that lower fund expenses are associated with higher returns.

3.3 Fund Performance

Chay and Trzcinka (1999) report a strong positive relationship between the level of a fund's premium and next year's NAV return.

3.4 Management Compensations

Coles, et al. (June 2000) find that fund discounts decline as the marginal compensation of managers rises.

3.5 Management Ownership

Barclay, et al. (1993) find that funds with managers holding large blocks of stock sell at larger discounts than those with lower ownership positions.

3.6 Restricted Stocks / Unrecognized Gains

Malkiel (1995) finds support for both the restricted stock and the unrecognized capital gains hypotheses.

3.7 Market Efficiency

Pontiff (November 1996) employs a multifactor model and finds support for a number of frictions associated with fund discounts. The model explains about 20% of discount variability.

Pontiff (March 1997) finds that funds shares are 64% more volatile than NAV and concludes that the market efficient hypothesis does not hold.

4. IDIOSYNCRATIC STUDIES

4.1 Trading Strategies / Mean Reversion

Pontiff (1995) reports that the primary source of returns to fund trading strategies is the mean-reverting nature of discounts.

Arak, and Taylor (1996) use a discount based trading-filter model to switch money from a portfolio of foreign stocks to a respective country fund, etc., and report that the strategy outperforms a buy-and-hold strategy.

Arak and Taylor (1996) find support for the supposition that closed-end country funds violate the arbitrage profit rule.

Sias (Spring 1997) employs a weighted trading strategy based on discounts and finds that this results in higher returns than an equally-weighted strategy.

Olienyk, et al. (1999) report the possibility of arbitrage profits from predictable drifts between pairs of country funds.

4.2 IPO Papers

Peavy (May/June 1989) reports that closed-end fund IPOs begin trading at 7.54% premium to net asset value but decline to an average discount of 16% after 100 days.

Weiss Hanley, et al. (Spring 1996) conclude that closed-end fund IPO behavior is best explained by a "profitability to underwriters who market" hypothesis.

4.3 Theoretical Pieces

Schnabel (August 1992) uses an Arrow-Debreu state-preference model to explain why funds sell at discounts to NAV.

Chance (1997) demonstrates that closed-end fund discounts are a logical result from active portfolio management in an efficient market.

5. MANAGEMENT ISSUES

Porter, et al. (1999) finds that for repurchase announcements of closed-end funds, there is a positive relation between the amount of pre-announcement excess returns and the subsequent re-pricing of the shares.

Rowe and Davidson (August, 2000) report mixed findings of the impact that management changes have on the return performance of closed-end funds.

6. OTHER PAPERS

Close (1952) reports that a sample of closed-end funds' portfolios out-perform those of open-end funds.

Marcus and Yaari (Autumn 1988) argue that under certain circumstances, a closed-end fund can out-perform its own portfolio.

Caks and Zarruk. (Spring/Summer 1993) develop a model to explain how fund expenses can cause fared shares to sell at discount.

Peavy (1995) finds that returns to closed-end fund shareholders are positing in the first few days of January.

Neal and Wheatley (1998) investigate the adverse-selection of the bid-ask spread due to information asymmetry and find a smaller impact than those reported in other studies.

Lofthouse (Spring 1999) compares British investment trusts with U.S. funds and argues, among other things, that a lack of an arbitrage activity impacts trust discounts and by extension fund discounts.

Bers and Madura (August 2000) report that equity funds and taxable bond funds exhibit strong portfolio return persistence.

Chapter 9

CONCLUSION

Over the past decades different arguments have been offered to explain the magnitude of and/or behavior of closed-end fund discounts. Many of these arguments have been discarded or mitigated. We are reminded of the words of Richard McEnally, who, when referring to a different controversy in the finance literature stated, "Just because someone says it's so, many times, doesn't make it so."

However, in spite of false starts and partial successes, there have been numerous interesting findings about closed-end funds in the fifty years that have passed since the publication of the first academic study on these companies. We close this second volume much as we did our first -- with a broad-brush review of research findings about closed-end funds over the past decade.

The issue of investor sentiment and closed-end fund pricing was very popular during the period. Earlier studies such as Lee, et al. (1990) and De Long, et al. (1991) argued forcefully that fund discounts are significantly impacted by noise traders. A number of other studies such as Brauer (1993) and Chen, et al. (1993) frequently took issue with the sentiment hypothesis and offered supporting evidence for their position. Interestingly, one study reports that institutional trading activity in fund shares far exceeds what was previously believed. This finding is inconsistent with the lack of institutional activity assumption held by those who purport the validity of a noise trader model. This debate continues and almost certainly will be the subject of future studies.

A second area of investigation popular during the last decade involved closed-end country funds. Studies such as Bosner-Neal, et al. (1990) show that country fund share price premiums to net asset value are positively associated with the degree of foreign investor restrictions characterizing the fund's target market. Other studies such as Arshanapalli, et al. (1996) report that country fund returns are influenced by both target market return and the U.S. market return. Yet, others such as Chang, et al. (1995) report that country funds can yield diversification benefits for U.S. investors although they do not perfectly mirror their target market indexes.

A third area of investigation re-examines and expands the earlier research investigating rational explanations for fund discounts. Several studies find support for tax impacts, as well as for expense impacts on fund pricing. Newer interesting areas of investigation address the impact of management issues and fund performance on fund pricing.

Other studies address theoretical issues concerning closed-end funds, fund IPOs, and trading strategies. There is strong evidence that returns to investors who purchase fund IPOs are usually dismal. Strategy studies suggest that returns on closed-end fund shares exhibit a small amount of positive serial correlation, as do changes in closed-end fund discounts. In addition, there is growing evidence that the size of closed-end fund discounts is related to the future portfolio performance of the fund.

REFERENCES

Abraham, Abraham, Don Elan, and Alan J. Marcus. "Does Sentiment Explain Closed-End Fund Discounts? Evidence from Bond Funds." *Financial Review* 28.4 (November 1998): 609-619.

Anderson, Seth C. "Closed-End Funds versus Market Efficiency." *Journal of Portfolio Management* (Fall 1986): 63-67.

Anderson, Seth C. and Jeffery A. Born. Closed-End Investment Companies: Issues and Answers. Hingham, MA, Kluwer Academic Publishers, 1991.

Anderson, Seth C., Jay Coleman, Jeff Steagall, and Cheryl Frohlich. "A Multi-Factor Analysis of Country Fund Returns." *Journal of Financial Research* 24.3 (Fall 2001): 331-346.

Arak, Marcelle, and Dean Taylor. "Risk and Return in Trading Closed-End Funds: Can Trading Beat Holding Foreign Stocks?" *The Quarterly Review of Economics and Business* 36.2 (1996): 219-231.

Arak, Marcelle, and Dean Taylor. "Optimal Trading and Mean-Reverting Prices: Switching Between Foreign Stocks and Closed-End Country Funds." *Applied Economics* 28 (1996): 1067-74.

Arshanapalli, Bala, Jongmo Jay Choi, E. Tyler Clagget, Jr., John Doukas, and Insup Lee. "Explaining and Premiums and Discounts on Closed-End Equity Country Funds." *Journal of Applied Corporate Finance* 9.3 (Fall 1996): 109-117.

Bailey, Warren and Joseph Lim. "Evaluating the Diversification of New Country Funds." *Journal of Portfolio Management* (Spring 1992): 74-80.

Barclay, Michael J., Clifford G. Holderness, and Jeffrey Pontiff. "Private Benefits from Block Ownership and Discounts on Closed-End Funds." *Journal of Financial Economics* 33 (1993): 263-291.

Beckaert, Geert and Michael S. Urias. "Diversification, Integration and Emerging Market Closed-End Funds." *Journal of Finance* 51.3 (July 1996): 835-869.

Bers, Martina K. and Jeff Madura. "The Performance Persistence of Closed-End Funds." *Financial Review* 35.3 (August 2000): 33-52.

Bodurtha, James N. Jr., Dong-Soon Kim, and Charles M.C. Lee. "Closed-End Country Funds and U.S. Market Sentiment." *Review of Financial Studies* 8.3 (1995): 879-919.

Bosner-Neal, Catherine, Greggory A. Brauer, Robert Neal and Simon Wheatley. "International Restrictions and Closed-End Country Fund Prices." *Journal of Finance* 45.2 (June 1990): 523-547.

Brauer, Greggory A. "Open-Ending Closed-End Funds." *Journal of Financial Economics* 13.4 (December 1984): 491-507.

Brauer, Greggory A. "Investor Sentiment and the Closed-End Fund Puzzle: A 7 Percent Solution." *Journal of Financial Services Research* 7.2 (1993): 199-216.

Brickley, James, Steve Manaster, and James Schallheim. "The Tax Timing Option and the Discounts on Closed-End Investment Companies." *Journal of Business* 64.3 (1991): 287-312.

Brown, Gregory W. "Volatility, Sentiment, and Noise Traders" *Financial Analysts Journal* 55.2 (March/April 1999): 82-90.

Caks, John and Emilio R. Zarruk. "Closed-End Fund Discounts: Pedagogical Notes." *Financial Practice and Education* 3.1 (Spring/Summer 1993): 95-97.

Chance, Don M. "A Theory of the Value of Active Investment Management and its Implications for Closed-End Funds and Investment Management Contracts." *Advances in Financial Economics* 3.2 (1997): 81-115.

Chang, Eric, Cheol S. Eun, and Richard Kolodny. "International Diversification Through Closed-End Funds." *Journal of Banking and Finance* 19.4 (1995): 1237-63.

Chay, J. B. and Charles A. Trzcinka. "Managerial performance and the cross-sectional pricing of closed-end funds." *Journal of Financial Economics* 39.2 (1999): 379-408.

Chen, Nai Fu, Richard Roll and Stephen Ross. "Economic Forces and the Stock Market." *Journal of Business* 59.3 (1986): 383-404.

Chen, Nai Fu, Raymond Kan and Merton H. Miller. "Are the Discounts on Closed-End Funds a Sentiment Index?" *Journal of Finance* 48.2 (June 1993): 795-800.

Chen, Nai Fu, Raymond Kan and Merton H. Miller. "A Rejoinder." *Journal of Finance* 48.2 (June 1993): 809-810.

Choi, Jongmoo Jay and Insup Lee. "Market Segmentation and the Valuation of Closed-End Country Funds." *Review of Quantitative Finance and Accounting* 7.1 (1996): 45-63.

Chopra, Navin, Charles M.C. Lee, Andrei Shleifer, and Richard Thaler. "Yes, Discounts on Closed-End Funds Are A Sentiment Index." *Journal of Finance* 48.2 (June 1993): 801-808.

Chopra, Navin, Charles M.C. Lee, Andrei Shleifer, and Richard Thaler. "Summing-Up." *Journal of Finance* 48.2 (June 1993): 811-812.

Chowdhury, Abdur R. 'The Behavior of Closed-End Country Fund Prices in the Asian NIEs." *Applied Economic Letters* 1 (1994): 219-222.

Coles, Jeffery, Jose Suay, and Denise Woodbury. "Fund Advisor Compensation and Closed-End Funds." *Journal of Finance* 55.3 (June 2000): 1385-1414.

Close, James A. "Investment Companies: Closed-End versus Open-End." *Harvard Business Review* 30 (1952): 79-88.

De Long, J. Bradford, Andrei Shleifer, Larrence H. Summers and Richard J. Waldman. "Noise Trader Risk in Financial Markets." *Journal of Political Economy* 98 (1990): 703-738.

De Long, J. Bradford, Andrei Shleifer, Larrence H. Summers and Richard J. Waldman. "The Stock Market Bubble of 1929: Evidence from Closed-End Funds." *Journal of Economic History* 51.3 (September 1991): 675-700.

De Long, J. Bradford, Andrei Shleifer, Larrence H. Summers and Richard J. Waldman. "Closed-End Fund Discounts: A Yardstick of Small-Investor Sentiment." *Journal of Portfolio Management* 18.2 (Winter 1992): 46-53.

Errunza, Vihang, Lemma Senbet, and Ked Hogan. "The Pricing of Country Funds from Emerging Markets: Theory and Evidence." *International Journal of Theoretical and Applied Finance* 1.1 (1998): 111-143.

Fama, Eugene and Kenneth R. French. "Common Risk Factors in the Returns on Stocks and Bonds." *Journal of Financial Economics* 33.1 (1993): 3-56.

French, Kenneth R. and Richard Roll. "Stock Return Variances: The Arrival of Information and the Reaction of Traders." *Journal of Financial Economics* 17.1 (1986): 5-26.

Gibbons, Michael R. "Multivariate Tests of Financial Models: A New Approach." *Journal of Financial Economics* 10.1 (1982): 3-27.

Ghose, Subrata and Jeffery A. Born. "Asian and Latin American Emerging Market Closed-End Funds: Return and Diversification." *Emerging Markets Quarterly* 2.2 (Fall 1998): 63-75.

Johnson, Gordon, Thomas Schneeweis, and William Dinning. "Closed-End Country Funds: Exchange Rate and Investment Risk." *Financial Analysts Journal* 49.6 (November/December 1993): 74-82.

Kim, Chang-Soo. "Investor Tax-Trading Opportunities and Discounts on Closed-End Mutual Funds." *Journal of Financial Research* 17.1 (Spring 1994): 65-75.

Klibanoff, Peter, Owen Lamont, and Thierry A. Wizman. "Investor Reaction to Salient News in Closed-End Country Funds." *Journal of Finance* 52.2 (April 1998): 673-699.

Kramer, Charles and R. Todd Smith. "The Mexican Crisis and the Behavior of Country Fund Discounts: Renewing the Puzzle of Closed-End Fund Pricing." *International Journal of Theoretical and Applied Finance* 1.1 (1998): 164-171.

Kumar, Raman and Gregory M. Noronha. "A Re-Examination of the Relationship Between Closed-End Fund Discounts and Expenses." *Journal of Financial Research* 15.2 (Summer 1992): 139-147.

La Barge, Karin P. and Richard A. La Barge. "Portfolio Sets for Latin American Closed-End Country Funds in the Changing Interest Rate Environment of 1992-1994." *Journal of Financial Engineering* 5.1 (1996): 37-52.

Lee, Charles M. C. and Mark A. Ready. "Inferring Trade Direction from Intra-day Data." *Journal of Finance* 46.2 (May 1991): 733-746.

Lee, Charles M. C., Andrei Shleifer, and Richard H. Thaler. "Anomalies: Closed-End Fund Mutual Funds." *Journal of Economic Perspectives* 4.4 (Fall 1990): 154-64.

Lee, Charles M. C., Andrei Shleifer, and Richard H. Thaler. "Investor Sentiment and the Closed-End Fund Puzzle." *Journal of Finance* 66.1 (March 1991): 75-109.

Leonard, David C. and David M. Shull. "Investor Sentiment and the Closed-End Fund Evidence: Impact of the January Effect." *The Quarterly Review of Economics and Business* 36.1 (Spring 1996): 117-126.

Lofthouse, Stephen. "Closed-End Fund and Investment Trust Discounts." *Journal of Investing* 8.1 (Spring 1999): 27-37.

Malhotra, D. K. and Robert W. McLeod. "Closed-End Fund Expenses and Investment Selection." *Financial Review* 41.1 (Spring 2000): 85-104.

Malkiel, Burton. "The Valuation of Closed-End Investment Company Shares." *Journal of Finance* 32.2 (September 1977): 847-859.

Malkiel, Burton "The Structure of Closed-End Fund Discounts Revisited." *Journal of Portfolio Management* (Summer 1995): 32-38.

Marcus, Matityahu and Uzi Yaari. "How a Closed-End Fund Can Out-Perform Its Own Stock Portfolio." *International Journal of Finance* 1.1 (Autumn 1988): 1-14.

Medewitz, Jeanette N. Fuad A. Adullah, and Keith Olsen. "An Investigation into the Market Valuation Process of Closed-End Country Funds." *FM Letters* 23.1 (Spring 1994): 13-14.

Merton, Robert. "Options Pricing when Underlying Stock Returns are Discontinuous." *Journal of Financial Economics* 3 1/2 (1976): 125-144.

Miller, Edward M. "Rick, Uncertainty, and Divergence of Opinion." *Journal of Finance* 32.4 (December 1977): 1151-68.

Miller, Edward M. "Uncertainty Induced Bias in Capital Budgeting." *Financial Management* 7.3 (Fall 1978): 12-18.

Miller, Edward M. "Explaining Intra-Day and Overnight Price Behavior." *Journal of Portfolio Management* 15.4 (1989): 10-17.

Miller, Merton H. and Franco Modigliani. "Dividend Policy, Growth and the Valuation of Shares." *Journal of Business* 34.3 (October 1961): 411-33.

Neal, Robert and Simon M. Wheatley. "Do Measures of Investor Sentiment Predict Returns?" *Journal of Financial and Quantitative Analysis* 33.4 (December 1998): 523-547.

Neal, Robert and Simon M. Wheatley. "Adverse Selection and Bid-Ask Spreads: Evidence From Closed-End Funds." *Journal of Financial Markets* 1 (1998): 121-149.

Noronha, Gregory M. and Bruce L. Rubin. "Closed-End Bond Fund Discounts: Agency Costs, Investor Sentiment and Portfolio Content." *Journal of Economics and Finance* 19.3 (Summer 1995): 29-44.

Olienyk, John P., Robert Schweback, and J. Kenton Zumwalt. "WEBS, SPDRs, and Country Funds: An Analysis of International Co integration." *Journal of Multinational Finance* 9 (1999): 217-232.

Peavy John W. III. "Closed-End Fund IPOs: Caveat Emptor." *Financial Analysts Journal* 45.3 (May/June 1989): 71-75.

Peavy John W. III. "New Evidence on the Turn-of-the-Year Effect From Closed-End Fund IPOs." *Journal of Financial Research* 9.1 (1995): 49-64.

Pontiff, Jeffrey. "Closed-End Fund Premia and Returns: Implications for Financial Market Equilibrium." *Journal of Financial Economics* 37.2 (1995): 341-370.

Pontiff, Jeffrey. "Costly Arbitrage: Evidence From Closed-End Fund Discounts." *Quarterly Journal of Economics* 107 (November 1996): 1135-51.

Pontiff, Jeffrey. "Excess Volatility of Closed-End Funds." *American Economic Review* 87.1 (March 1997): 155-67.

Porter, Gary, Rodney L. Roenfeldt, and Neil W. Sicherman. "The Value of Open Market Repurchases of Closed-End Fund Shares." *Journal of Business* 72.2 (1999): 257-276.

Richards, Malcolm, Donald R. Fraser and John C. Groth. "Winning Strategies for Closed-End Funds." *Journal of Portfolio Management* 7.1 (Fall 1980): 50-55.

Rowe, Wei Wang and Wallace N. Davidson III. "Fund Manager Succession in Closed-End Mutual Funds." *Financial Review* 35.3 (August, 2000): 53-78.

Schnabel, Jacques A. "Corporate Spin-Offs and Closed-End Funds in a State-Preference Framework." *Financial Review* 27.3 (August 1992): 391-409.

Shiller, Robert. J. "Stock Prices and Social Dynamics," *Brooking Papers on Economic Activity*, (Fall 1984): 457-498.

Shiller, Robert J., "Speculative Prices and Popular Models," *Journal of Economic Perspectives* (Spring 1990): 55-65.

Sias, Richard. "The Sensitivity of Individual and Institutional Investors' Expectations to Changing Market Conditions: Evidence From Closed-End Funds." *Review of Quantitative Finance and Accounting* 8.1 (1997): 245-69.

Sias, Richard. "Price Pressure and the Role of Institutional Investors in Closed-End Funds." *Journal of Financial Research* 20.2 (Summer 1997): 211-229.

Sias, Richard. "Optimum Trading Strategies for Closed-End Funds." *Journal of Investing* 6.1 (Spring 1997): 54-61.

Swaminathan, Bhaskaran. "Time-Varying Expected Small Firm Returns and Closed-End Fund Discounts." *Review of Financial Studies* 9.3 (1996): 845-887.

Thompson, Rex. "The Information Content of Discounts and Premiums on Closed-End Fund Shares." *Journal of Financial Economics* 6.2 (June 1978): 151-186.

Weiss Hanley, Kathleen, Charles M.C. Lee, and Paul J. Sequin. "The Marketing of Closed-End Fund IPOs: Evidence from Transaction Data." *Journal of Financial Intermediation* 5.1 (Spring 1996): 127-159.

Index

MIX
Papier aus verantwortungsvollen Quellen
Paper from responsible sources
FSC® C105338

FSC
www.fsc.org

If you have any concerns about our products,
you can contact us on
ProductSafety@springernature.com

In case Publisher is established outside the EU,
the EU authorized representative is:
Springer Nature Customer Service Center GmbH
Europaplatz 3, 69115 Heidelberg, Germany

Printed by Libri Plureos GmbH
in Hamburg, Germany